A Mother's
NIGHTMARE

A Mother's
NIGHTMARE

the building of a case

BRENDA AVANT

Outskirts Press, Inc.
Denver, Colorado

Article originally published in the Daily Commercial, July 1991

Outskirts Press, Inc.
http://www.outskirtspress.com

ISBN: 978-1-4327-7063-1

Outskirts Press and the "OP" logo are trademarks belonging to Outskirts Press, Inc.

PRINTED IN THE UNITED STATES OF AMERICA

In Loving Memories of my mother
Estella Avant
And my sister Merdis Taylor

Nothing is as precious
As the love a mother
Has for her child

Acknowledgements

I would like to thank all of my family, friends, co-workers
and doctors for all the letters, testimonies, encouragement
and
Support during this difficult time

Contents

A Mother's Nightmare

I STILL SHED tears every now and then when I think of what happened, reliving the nightmare. It's strange how a person plans his or her life and within an instance an event can occur and change that person's entire life. I am that such person. I thought at one point in my life I had it all planned out. My path would be a straight one; I would bypass all the obstacles that could potentially block my path. I had goals, and every goal was in order. I planned to accomplish those goals. I was not going to give people the opportunity to predetermine my life, expecting me to be or behave a certain way, to label me. I was determined not to fall into that stereotype line. The very thing I had hoped to avoid was what I encountered.

I, like many other women, reached a point in my life where I had a desire to settle down from my busy lifestyle. So after spending years in the military, I completed my enlistment, returned to my home state, got a job working as a licensed practical nurse, enrolled in nursing school, completed my degree in nursing, became a registered nurse. During this phase of my life, it dawned on me that my biological clock was ticking, and it made me aware that my life as I imagined it was not complete; I wanted a child.

Introduction

I WRITE THIS story for different reasons. First, I want people in this country, the land of the free, to be aware of the fact that we are living in a country that professes there is liberty and justice for all, but such is so far from the truth.

Second, I want to share my experience, my hurt, in a therapeutic way with others who may have experienced similar situations so that I may be supportive in some way.

I'm aware, just as many others, that child abuse does exist and is becoming more prevalent in this country and more so since I started writing my story some nine years ago, but I'm also aware of the many falsely accused cases that are just as devastating as the true cases themselves.

I never could make sense of the statement that's still being used today and was used more times than I cared to remember, "Err on the side of the child."There's no room for error on any side. It's like executing someone, then finding out later that person was innocent. How does one rectify that? In a way, I felt as though I was actually being executed. I was dying inside. It was as if I wanted to will my heart to stop beating, so the hurt would go away, but somewhere deep inside I knew I had to live so that I could fight to get my son back.

I suffered financially, physically, and emotionally. This

traumatic experience dealt with my pride, my dignity. It invaded my privacy, took away my constitutional rights. I had no freedom of speech. Many of the words I spoke were used against me. Definitions gained new meanings. Words were conveniently perceived as necessary to build a case. This ordeal took total control in every aspect of my life, but through it all, I managed to maintain my sanity, though at times I felt as if it was slipping away from me. I survived with the help of a greater power. I held on to my belief, my faith, that eventually the truth would become known and consequently would set me free. It is said in this country that one is presumed innocent until proven guilty. Well, this didn't apply to me, and I'm sure that I speak for the many others who have had such experiences. My verdict was guilty, and it was up to me to prove my innocence.

Proving my innocence was more difficult than I ever could have imagined, not only in the courtroom, but in the eyes of the public as well.

It amazes me how quickly people jump to conclusions, so easily to believe something negative, to pass judgment especially when it comes to the issue of children.

Many people believe what is presented to them, through the media or word of mouth, not taking the time to realize that in many cases the truth is often twisted.

This reminded me of a game we played in elementary school where a rumor started at the front of the class; a student started by whispering something to another student, and it was passed from student to student until it finally ended up to the last student repeating what he or she had heard.

It was always different from the words the rumor started with. Somewhere down the line someone added on, gave the rumor something negative to add to the excitement. After all, bad news travel faster than good news, and definitely gains more attention. So therefore, I had to work hard to prove my innocence to try and get rid of the guilty verdict, to try to convince the negative believer of the truth, though I knew there would always be some who thrive off negativity and refuse to accept the truth, those who like passing the rumor.

Throughout my life, I had heard the expression, "we live, and we learn," and I have indeed. I have lived, learned, experienced, and have become aware of the true society that we live in. I never imagined that I would be a victim of racism with damaging results; I never imagined that I would be in a courtroom trying to prove my innocence. I never imagined a man having the power and control to transform a mother's love into a mother's nightmare.

Childhood

EVEN AS A child, I was somewhat different from my siblings and friends. I would joke that perhaps I was from another planet, an alien of some sort, but the truth of the matter was I was from this planet, but alienated myself under certain circumstances.

I didn't share many of the beliefs others had. I perceived things differently, and I tried to see the good in what others saw as bad. It wasn't until years later that I realized I had inherited these traits from my mother.

Although I was raised in a predominantly Black community in the good ole South, and in an era where prejudice was as obvious as the rising of the sun, I refused to let such evil and ignorance enter the peaceful environment I had created within myself. Therefore, in my spare time I would occupy myself with reading whatever material I found interesting at the time, writing poems, short stories, keeping my dairy updated, and visiting the elderly, listening to age- old tales, trying to ingest the knowledge, the wisdom.

Perhaps I was naive or it was just a form of denial, but I refused to believe that racism existed to the extreme as I had heard others speak of. I often thought that people exaggerated. Was it possible for people to harbor such hate because of a person's skin color, race, or whatever the makeup that differentiates us one from another?

Although I wasn't completely ignorant to the fact, I knew it actually did exist to some extent, because I, too, had experienced some form of prejudice while attending the newly integrated high school, but nothing major, at least I didn't think so at the time because the problem was resolved fairly quickly. I didn't become aware of the seriousness of it until years later when I finally realized what could have and would have happened had the issue not been resolved. So, therefore, I suppose I stored it away in my subconscious mind, perhaps with the thought or hope that it would just go away, but unfortunately, it didn't. I came to realize that ignorance just doesn't fade away, and prejudice is indeed a form of ignorance.

I suppose I was a prime example of someone who had sight, but was so blind that I couldn't see that there was indeed a black and a white. I would never have imagined in my wildest dreams that I would experience first-hand the vicious bite of prejudice.

I grew up in a large close-knit family, fourteen other siblings to be exact, my twin and I being number twelve and thirteen. My father, a minister, and my mother were separated at some point during my childhood. My mother carried on portraying the role as mother and father. We worked together and learned to survive together.

Although my mother had no degree, what she taught us and embedded into our minds was beyond anything that existed in any textbook. She instilled in us morals and values she thought necessary to survive the many obstacles we would perhaps face in life. She had a way of teaching us by giving examples of situations people encountered in life and the consequences they had to pay for actions and choices they made. She simply believed in doing what was right. She would say to us, "If you lie, you will cheat and steal." Basically, she believed if a person lied, he or she was capable of doing anything immoral. My mother simply did not tolerate lies. It was best to tell the truth and deal with the consequences. We abided by her words.

Even though we were poor, I don't think we realized it, because at the time and, perhaps still today, people believe being poor is synonymous with hunger and uncleanness. Fortunately neither applied to us. There was a time when I was younger that we didn't have electricity, so therefore we had no utilities of our own. I remember us having to share the faucet and pump with our neighbor. We would carry water daily for the use of cooking and bathing. We weren't allowed to go to bed dirty, so we boiled the water on the wood stove, then transferred it to a tin tub where we took our bath.

I don't ever remember experiencing hunger. My mother managed to have a hot meal for us every day. During my adulthood, I heard my sister, who's older, say there were times when my mother made a meal out of water and flour, using the only ingredients she had to make bread and gravy. As a young child, one doesn't realize these things. When it was time to eat, food was always available. When I look back, I know my mother made many sacrifices and no doubt deprived herself of many things, perhaps even food for herself.

We had such love and togetherness in our large family. We benefited in many ways by working together. We learned to ration and utilize what we had sparely. Of course, it wasn't unusual to experience some rough days, and in our cases, more than most families; not rough in the sense of being hungry or in desperate need, but in the sense of not having what other families had financially, which, of course, limited some of our needs and definitely our wants.

I don't recall asking for much of anything during my childhood unless it was something needful; we all knew our finances were limited. Though some families didn't suffer financially as we did, they suffered in other ways. Many didn't have the love, the closeness we shared which actually made them envious of us, which I didn't understand, until I got older, that money couldn't buy happiness. We had priceless possessions, things that money couldn't buy.

On one of those days when things were a little rough, I remember saying to my sister after she voiced her words of discouragement one day, "If we didn't go through the bad times, we wouldn't know how to appreciate the good times." I was hoping my words of encouragement would make her feel better and at the same time secretly convincing myself in believing the words I had spoken.

At some stage in my life, I thought that one day I'd like to follow in my mother's footstep, have fifteen children. I observed her strength, her ability to maintain control. She didn't seem to worry, to stress herself. She made it all look so easy, so enjoyable, but as I grew older, I grew wiser. I realized I could never be the woman my mother was. She was a remarkable woman.

Later in life when I was truly old enough to understand, I realized raising fifteen children alone was difficult for my mother, and she endured worry and stress, but this remarkable mother concealed it. She refused to let her children see her shed a tear unless it was a tear of joy. I felt fortunate and blessed that I was given the opportunity to receive such guidance and have strong values instilled, not only from my mother, but from the elderly in the community as well, whom

I often visited. With this powerful combination, I had the tools I needed to face the world. I knew when I had a child one day I would give to him or her what my mother had given to me and would utilize the knowledge I had gained from my respected sources.

I was an observer, a listener, often hearing people stereotype, expecting people to behave or act a certain way because of race. I was determined not to fall into that stereotype line. I wanted people to see and judge me if they felt the need to do so as an individual, not because of my race.

As I started getting older, I experienced racism on different occasion, but not once did I succumb to such ignorance.

We didn't integrate into the school system until I was in the eighth grade. Racial tension was high and all around. I tried to avoid it, not put myself in that hostile environment. However now, in the eighth grade, I was provoked by a white boy, all because he didn't want my locker near his; the reason, because I was black. I responded in a negative manner. Afterward I felt terrible. I knew this was out of my character. Instead of anger, I actually felt sadness, perhaps because I was disappointed that race was still such an issue. I think I was hoping deep inside that now things would be different, that some changes had come about since we had integrated the school and disappointed in myself because I stooped to his level.

As time passed, I had to face reality. We were indeed living in an era where people were still being judged by the color of their skin.

I had to experience it first- hand, the most serious and fearful thing that happened during my childhood. I was accused of beating a white girl. Besides the girl being white, which was a problem within itself in this town filled with hatred and prejudice, she was from a prominent family, so needless to say, these people had a lot of influence.

I remember a police officer coming to our house at night, which was unusual, because we never had police come to our house and found it odd that he would show up in the nighttime.

When my mother answered the door she was surprised to see him standing there and was shocked when she heard the reason why, accusing me of an assault. When my mother told me the police officer came for me and I had to go with him, I was puzzled and somewhat afraid.

I was perhaps around fifteen and too naïve to be as fearful at the time as my mother was, because I knew the truth and simply thought the truth would set me free. After all, my mother had always taught us about honesty and the positive outcome. My mother, on the other hand, also knew the truth. She knew I couldn't have done such a thing, but she knew the truth didn't always set one free, especially when it dealt with race, especially in those days and in the good ole South and in that town.

That town was once part of the town I grew up in. The towns were divided because of racism and prejudice. The tragedy started before I was born and ended when I was old enough to remember.

Many of my siblings and my mother remembered only too well, knowing some of the families and the four black males, one teenage boy age sixteen, two twenty-two years old, and a twenty-seven year old falsely accused of raping and abducting a married white woman.

Though there was no evidence of rape and all the accused whereabouts were accounted for, and the supposing abducted woman was at her home, accusations from a white woman was all needed. An all-white jury found them guilty. The results were literally a natural disaster, requiring assistance from the National Guard. False accusations resulted in a riot and one of the young men being killed by a deputized Klan posse, in which the sheriff was also involved.

After the riot, the guilty verdict remained. The teenage boy was given a life sentence and the other two the death penalty. Two years later the US Supreme court reversed the death penalty, and the two men were to have a new trial. The sheriff, known to be a racist, was transporting them back to this county for a new trial. He claimed he pulled off the road to check a flat tire and the handcuffed men left the police secured car and attacked him. He fired six shots, killing one and gravely wounding the other, thinking he, too, was dead. The one lived to tell the true story, that they were pulled from the car and shot in cold blood.

After many changes of events, the teenager, now a man, was paroled and moved to another state, making his whereabouts unknown to many. The man who was wounded survived and spend a total of nineteen years in prison before he was paroled, only to die the following year of a suspicious death while traveling home to visit his family.

So no doubt, this was why my mother worried. I'm sure it bought back memories of that dreadful time. Although she didn't expect that there would be anything as drastic as a riot again because there were now laws in place, she wasn't ignorant to the fact that there were people who got around the law or was the law, as in the case of the four males. She knew there could possibly be some trouble.

The police officer took us to the home of the girl I was accused of beating so that she could identify me. I suppose from there, depending on her answer, I was going to be taken to jail, or wherever he would decide to take me. As a child, it never dawned on me that this wasn't normal procedure for a police officer to take matters into his own hands. I actually never thought at the time about what would or could have happened to me had she identified me as the one who assaulted her.

I know my mother thanked God and sighed a breath of relief when she heard the girl say, "No, she's not the one, she's a nice person." Someone had gone out of her way to provide my name and any other information that was helpful in identifying me after she had beaten the girl. Eventually they found out who she was. I never understood why the girl had chosen me to accuse or the reason for her fighting the girl. I don't think it was because of anything the girl had done. I think perhaps she was targeted because of her status, and she knew attacking her would be major trouble for the individual performing the act, in this case me.

All I could think of was envy. The girl was a loner without many friends, if any, and some people were cruel to her. I was the opposite, with many friends, and well liked. If only she had known my desire to befriend her and my dislike of the way others treated her. I actually felt sorry for her that she would go to such extremes, so I never confronted her about the situation. I just erased it from my mind, perhaps because of empathy and being so young, so therefore I didn't feel the hurt, anger, or fear of being accused of something I knew I hadn't done.

I never knew exactly what ever happened to that girl; no one ever talked about it again. I was sent back home after the victim told the police officer I was innocent. I don't think I thought about it again for many years. I am not sure; I could say the same for my mother. Perhaps the fear lingered for a while, but she never made it known.

While other children attended after school activities, we were working in the fields, orange groves, or any other legitimate job that provided us with an income. My mother cleaned houses, but also joined us, worked right beside us as we labored in the field. Of course, being a child, at times, I wanted to participate in certain activities as well as my siblings, but even at that age, there was unselfishness about us as we watched our mother struggle. We knew there was no extra money for such activities. Our priority was survival, and we had to survive as a family. Therefore, we all fulfilled our duties and obligations. We worked together, and the money we earned was given to my mother to help in whatever way the money was needed; however, she would still make the sacrifice and give us some of the earnings, though she needed it.

I remembered a time I so desperately searched for a quarter for a hayride, just a fun activity where children rode on the hay in the back of a truck. I knew my mother couldn't afford to give it to me because it would have meant her trying to provide for the other siblings as well, so needless to say there was no hayride, but no bitterness. I understood that the money was needed for something else more important. We knew at an early age what responsibility was all about.

There are times that I reminisce about my childhood and ask myself many times, how did we survive under such circumstances? Each time the answers are the same--God, my mother, determination, love, strength, togetherness, endurance.

During my childhood into my teenage years, we did without many things. Though I went through some hard times, it didn't compare to what my mother and older siblings had to endure. For many years, there was a time when we had no electricity; not that it was turned off due to not paying the utility bill, *We had no electricity.* I remember having to use kerosene lamps for light and many years of having to use a wood stove for cooking and heat. My mother had to pay the neighbors for use of their faucet, where we filled buckets with water for cooking and bathing.

We never had a car during my entire childhood. My mother never learned to drive. We had outdoors toilets, and a house that leaked when it rained.

Many people observed our lifestyle and pitied us, but the reality of it all was that we were actually happy, because this was a way of life for us. We knew no other life, and we definitely couldn't miss what we never had.

Though we spent many hours working, we had a balanced life. There were plenty of playtimes, even if it was mostly among ourselves. It was happy times, which allowed us to build upon and strengthen the bond between us, spending quality time, having morals, and values instilled.

My mother would say, "Where there's a will, there's a way," and it was evident because though we didn't have electricity to provide us with light, heat, air, or an electric or gas stove to cook, or running water; we still kept clean, warm, had hot meals, had lighted areas, and fresh air to breathe. We didn't have a car, but we got where we needed to go.

Through hard work and determination over the years, we were finally able to obtain the necessities to be qualified as living modern--a gas stove, our own electricity, water, even an indoor bathroom.

As years passed, we had many memories and laughs about our outdoor toilet. I remembered the teenage years into young adulthood of the embarrassing moments when company would come, especially boys, and ask to use the bathroom. We younger girls would always have an excuse as to why they couldn't use it. We would tell the guest it was in use, but our older sister would say, "Go straight out to the back of the house." Although embarrassed, we had to laugh at her directness. Through it all, it was a childhood to remember, with many fond memories.

Military

THE REMAINDER OF my childhood was basically uneventful. We had to survive as a family, so we all pulled together, worked, and fulfilled our obligations. We had rules, and we abided by them. Not once, did my mother have to enter a courthouse or a jail due to any crime committed. We had the utmost respect for her. We were determined not to cause any unnecessary stress in her life.

My mother was such a giving person, willing to share what little she had. I felt I needed to give back to her. I worked jobs to make a living, but had no contentment. I was not making enough money to help my mother as I wanted. I wanted to continue my education, but didn't have the finances to attend college, and my mother had done her best. She made sure we got a high school education. I remember her saying that she couldn't afford to send us to college, but would make sure we finished high school. She laid the foundation and that was good enough for me, because I knew I could build upon it and set my goals from there. It was just a matter of getting the money to do so, and I knew in time I would. I wanted to travel, to see the world, or what part of the world I could see, but couldn't afford to do so.

One day I was reading a paper, and the solution was right

before my eyes, the words, "Travel and get an education-join the Army," and that's just what I did. Of course, I was somewhat naïve. I was surprised to know that I had other duties to perform other than traveling and getting an education. I had many laughs about this, but everything fell in place and worked out well for me.

I knew I made the right choice in joining the military. It taught me to be more responsible and gave me some stability. Prior to joining the military, I was still searching, moving places, but actually not getting anywhere. Here it wasn't so easy to just get up and move. One was somewhat forced to stay in place and make the best of it, not run away when things weren't working the way one wanted or thought it should be. It contributed to my maturity and growth. It allowed me the opportunity to travel, meet people from all lifestyles, which was beneficial to me. I learned to deal with and become aware of the different cultures, nationalities, ethnic backgrounds and personalities.

During my tour in Europe, I utilized most of my spare time traveling. I was constantly touring other countries every opportunity I got. I found great interest in other cultures, educating myself as I visited country after country, from the Buckingham Palace in London to the Keukenhof Gardens in Holland.

From each country, there was a story to tell. My favorite was when I was in Switzerland. I was sitting on a bench at a ski resort. People walked by staring at me in amazement. My first instinct was to look down at myself checking to see if my clothing was fasten or zipped, then it finally occurred to me that many of the natives had perhaps not seen a black person before. Then all of a sudden, a man approached me with his hands behind his back, and as he got closer, he slowly eased his hands from behind his back, snapped my picture with the camera he had concealed, and swiftly walked away.

I smiled and wasn't bothered by it. I knew he meant no harm; just curious. I wondered what he ever did with the photo.

When I exited the tour bus in Rome, people rubbed, touched my skin. I knew these people meant no harm. Much of their behavior was, too, out of curiosity.

I think one of the most interesting places that stimulated my awareness of the difference and the true society I was living in was my tour in England. When I was sightseeing and shopping, I remember walking into a shop hearing the voices with British accents before seeing the faces. I was amazed to turn around to see two dark-skinned women conversing. I realized my travels were more than pleasurable events, but educational as well.

Blacks and whites in England are recognized as British, they are not separated by race as black or white as in America where race is significant. The classification of race is so important in America until for many years the one-drop rule was put into place, a term uniquely used in the historical United States for the social classification as black of individuals with any African ancestry assigning mixed race people to an inferior race.

Somehow, there's a necessity, an importance to differentiate, for whatever reason. I personally don't understand and know of only a few reasons that are important or necessary to address one race. The most important reason I find it necessary is when medical studies or research are done concerning certain illnesses and diseases that affect people of certain race, so the awareness is there, giving people the opportunity to be proactive in seeking care as needed, and for medical

interventions. However, race is used for every statistic beginning from birth to death. I wonder what the true rationale is
for it all.

I was born here in America. I've lived among my fellow
Americans enough to know that we all are curious about certain things in life. However, my fellow Americans know what
dark skin looks like, no photo necessary, know my skin color
doesn't rub off when rubbed or touched, and know I bleed the
same color blood as they do, and know that if they are curious, they can just ask.

After two years in Germany, I returned to the states and
served for another three years. When I completed my tour in
the military I returned home alone, meaning without a military husband as some expected. I had dated in the military,
but it seemed as though I was always transferring to another
duty station, making it difficult for a sincere lasting relationship. So now that I was out, I thought it was time to focus on a
relationship with the possibility of marriage. Of course, I was
always selective. The man who would be my husband and the
father of my child had to possess certain qualities, and everything had to fit into my life plan.

I eventually met a man who was kind, compassionate,
and hard working, blond hair and blue eyes. Our difference in
skin color was never an issue. It was as though we were both
color blind and found the true understanding of the saying
that opposites attract; however, I still had goals to accomplish
before getting into a marriage and having children.

I wanted to complete my education, not only for the sake
of increasing my income, but to reap the benefits that education provides, both necessary for me to provide the lifestyle
and education I had planned for my future child.

I had known mothers who were unable to provide for their

children's needs. I couldn't begin to imagine the sadness, the hurt, the fear a mother experiences from not being able to do so. I was determined that I wasn't going to be caught in this predicament.

Motherhood

MY MIND GOES back to that November night, 1990, when I sat on the side of the bed and waited nervously for the results of my home pregnancy test. I had purchased the test kit months prior because I had finally decided that I wanted to have a baby.

I thought I had it all planned. I would graduate from nursing school that following May and have the baby three months later. I even planned the season; I didn't want to be pregnant when it was too hot or too cold.

I had thought long and hard before getting pregnant. I knew that time was of the essence, because my biological clock was ticking.

I think back to the time when a man whom I was conversing with was beyond surprised that I was in my thirties and had no children. He thought this to be unusual for a "Black woman." I had determined long before this conversation, during the time in my life when I was old enough to realize just what life was all about, that I wouldn't fall into that stereotype line. If people stereotyped me, it would be because of their ignorance, not facts.

I promised myself that I wouldn't have a child until I was financially able to provide for him or her, married or not, until

I was ready. Ready included knowing all about raising a child, giving up certain things in life that would interfere with motherhood, and the willingness to devote myself completely.

I had no doubt that I would be a good mother. After all, I had a wonderful role model, my mother. I knew what was instilled in me was that special something I could always utilize in raising my own child.

Once I had accomplished what I called the necessary requirements, I decided I was ready to make that commitment.

When I saw the positive sign, meaning I was pregnant, I didn't know whether to laugh or cry, to jump up or just sit there. I had to say it out loud so that I could believe it. I repeated over and over again, *I'm pregnant, I'm pregnant,* then I thought, who will I tell first, my boyfriend, my mother, my sisters; who?

It didn't take long before practically everybody who knew me heard of the news. Many were surprised because they never thought I'd get pregnant.

Even being an adult, I was a little reluctant to share the news with my mother, having a baby out of wedlock. My sister told her before I had the opportunity to do so, but to my surprise she was happy for me. If she ever had an opinion about it, she kept it to herself. She respected my decision. When my boyfriend heard the news, he was just as surprised as I was and happy to finally become a father.

I finally went to my Gynecologist to confirm my positive home test. My doctor and I had calculated the same date when my baby would be born. I did everything by the book and followed my doctor's advice. I wanted a healthy baby.

At first, it was as though I wasn't pregnant at all. I simply didn't feel anything different that other women talked about, and what I had read. I was beginning to wonder if this was all to being pregnant and what was *the big deal*. Around the second month, I was beginning to find out what the big deal was and was starting to "feel" pregnant. I was sick, of course, had the nausea and vomiting, but also had a condition called ptyalin-excessive salivation. I continued to work full-time on an evening shift and went to college during the day. I didn't have the nausea and vomiting every day, but I had the excessive salivation, which restricted me from going too many places and doing too many things. I remember my dear mother decorating a container so I could carry it with me so I wouldn't have to make numerous trips to the restroom.

My classmates and teachers gave me a wonderful baby shower. To my surprise, the college president attended. I think he admired my enthusiasm, my determination to continue my education regardless of my circumstance. My co-workers were also planning one for me, but this shower didn't take place until after the birth of my son.

I didn't have to buy many maternity clothes because I didn't show signs of pregnancy for many months. In fact, I wore the same size uniforms to work. But then it all happened so fast. By the sixth month, I was like a different person. I had gained sixty-five pounds. I knew that something was wrong. My dress sizes before pregnancy were threes and fives, shoe size eight. Under my cap and gown that graduation night in May, I wore a size twenty-two dress and a size ten shoe. I started to swell and have problems with my blood pressure.

I remembered a condition I had studied in my obstetrician class, pre-eclampsia-the development of high blood pressure, swelling, and spilling of protein into the urine, which could lead to the eclampsia state, resulting in seizures, convulsions, or coma. My doctor confirmed my suspicion. He put me on bed rest for a few days and allowed me to lie only on one side. I returned to the doctor's office and was immediately hospitalized. Although I didn't feel bad, just uncomfortable, my condition was getting worse. I started to spill protein in my urine. I was given a medication to prevent seizures, but soon had an allergic reaction to the medicine.

After a couple of days in that hospital, my doctor called to tell me that he was transferring me out to a hospital that specialized in my condition. The hospital that I was in was not equipped to take care of me. I was suddenly afraid for the life of my child. I cried uncontrollably as the staff hurriedly assisted me with getting dressed and put me on the stretcher. I had no time to call anyone, the doctor made sure my family was notified. I wasn't aware at the time the phone call was more than to inform them of my whereabouts, but my critical condition as well.

I was rushed to another hospital. I found myself unaware of what was going on. Before I knew what was happening, I found myself in a room with several people surrounding me, each working on different parts of my body; one starting an intravenous line for fluids and other medications that needed to be administered through my veins, one inserting a Foley catheter, one drawing blood from my other arm, the doctor doing an ultra sound.

I was shocked when a nurse approached me to tell me that I was going to have a baby at that moment. I had barely made it out of my sixth month.

The doctor couldn't guarantee that the baby would be all right. I cried even more. I never thought about the possibility of losing my life, which was possible at this point. I was only concerned about the life of my child.

I was given a spinal, a procedure where an anesthetic is inserted into the spinal canal to prevent movement or sensation below that level of the body, so that I could have an emergency Cesarean section, a surgical procedure to deliver a baby through the abdomen. Within minutes, I was carried off into the operating room, and in a short time, I had delivered a baby boy.

After my son was born, I remember seeing four or five people looking down at him in the basinet, which made me nervous and afraid. I wondered if something was wrong with him. I asked if he was all right and heard the answer yes. I wasn't sure if they were observing how small he was or that he looked white.

The last thing I remembered was telling the anesthesiologist that I couldn't breathe before I passed out. I had no idea how long I was out. When I opened my eyes, I was in another room, and my boyfriend was standing beside the bed.

My illness didn't go away after the birth of my son. I had a tube in my nose down to my stomach. I couldn't urinate on my own once the catheter was removed, so it had to be re-inserted. My blood pressure was at a critical high. I was receiving medication through the intravenous line. Days passed; I had yet to see my son. My boyfriend and hospital volunteers kept me updated on his condition. Since he was premature, he had minor medical issues needing attending to, but also needed to be under careful observation.

My boyfriend alternated his time between work and staying with us at the hospital as much as possible.

Finally, seven days later, I was taken down to see my baby. I will never forget that moment when I reached inside his crib to touch his tiny hand how he embraced my finger as if he knew I was his mother. That squeeze was the beginning of our bond. From that moment on, we were inseparable. When I wasn't with him in the flesh, he was with me in my mind and in my heart.

I had another surgery before leaving the hospital. I was finally released almost two weeks later. Needless to say, I was somewhat weak. I still had restrictions; it was difficult trying to do everything I needed to do in my condition, especially with a baby, so eventually my boyfriend moved in with me to help.

Our baby had a fair complexion. The only difference between him and his father was that his father had blond hair and blue eyes, and he had black hair and brown eyes. His skin was so light and transparent, one could see vein- like lines in his arms and legs.

One of the things that had often entered my mind and made me fearful over the years even before having a baby was the thought of crib death, when the baby is put down to sleep in his/her crib and later found dead, the most common cause of death among infants. It escalated when my son was born, because I knew it happened more in boy babies, especially with my baby being premature. I let my baby sleep in the basinet, because, of course, I was nervous with him sleeping with me. I kept the basinet close by the bed. Many nights I would sleep with my hands on him. This way I could feel his chest rise, knowing he was breathing. Eventually I was able to feel comfortable enough to not sleep with my hands on him, but made regular checks on him throughout the night.

Before I was a mother, I used to hear these mothers talking about different things their children had done and thought, what's so cute or special about that? Now I was doing the same thing. I was just like every other mother; I bragged or talked about every little thing I thought was cute and precious. There's a bond between a mother and a child that's indescribable. I had such a bond. I nurtured my son in every way. I did everything by the book and from the instructions of my pediatrician, even watched videos. Our baby only left our sight for short periods of time. He was always in the same room. If I was not watching him, his father was. We were finally getting in the swing of parenthood.

The time was getting closer for me to return to work. My six weeks that I was allowed after his birth was almost over. I had called several daycares trying to find the one I felt comfortable with after hearing so many horrible stories. I hated the thought of leaving him as it was, but knew I had to decide on one soon. I was definitely going to check it out thoroughly.

My life plan took an unexpected turn and started to unravel. I was asked to cover for a nurse at work on a weekend perhaps a week or so before I was to begin work. I decided to go on because I knew I had to do it eventually and needed to get used to leaving him.

His father babysat him on Saturday, but had to work on Sunday. I had many family members, including my mother, who would have been more than willing to babysit him, but my friend and neighbor whom I had met three years prior asked to babysit him, and since she was just a few minutes from my job and lived across the street, I decided to let her. I called several times from work to check on him, making sure everything was all right.

I couldn't wait until it was time to get off from work to get home to my baby. I thought of him constantly throughout the day. After all, this was the first time he had been with anyone besides his father and me. I just couldn't get to him fast enough. When I picked him up from my friend, I was relieved to know that he was fine, and everything went well.

Unfortunately, I later started having problems with my car; nothing major, but it had a problem that needed repairing. It was important to always have a car available, especially with the baby. My boyfriend had to drive to his job in the town he lived, so his car wasn't available. Instead of renting a car, my niece suggested I use her car while mine was being repaired.

Our night started uneventfully, and then the nightmare began. We had gotten the baby bathed and were watching television in the bedroom when a knock came on the door. I gave him to his father while I went to answer the door. It was my niece. She brought me her car. I thought her husband had followed her in his car to take her back home, but she had driven, so I had to take her home. She lived about a mile away.

We made a quick stop at a change machine for her to get some change in route to her house. I never got out of the car, I dropped her off and headed back home.

What happened next could have been something used against me in court had I spoken of it at the time. I was driving toward home and all of a sudden had the strangest feeling, something I cannot describe in words. It was a feeling of fear, a feeling that something was going to happen or had happened.

I remembered watching a television show with these mothers in different situations who talked about experiencing this same type of feeling when something had happened to their children. It bought back memories immediately, because I could now relate to these mothers. Perhaps this happened because the bond with my son was so strong.

I couldn't get home fast enough. As I got closer, my heart pounded. Before I could even park the car I noticed my boyfriend standing in the doorway with our son in his arms rocking him, yelling at me to hurry. I jumped out of the car with no memories of ever turning the ignition off.

I grabbed our baby and asked hysterically what had hap-pened, what was wrong. His father said he had fallen off the bed, that he had laid him on the bed while going to the refrig-erator to get some juice and heard a thump, ran into the room, and found him on the floor. We were always careful to place pillows around him before leaving him when he was lying in the big bed because, regardless of the books written on what age a baby is capable of doing different activities, movement in particular, I as a mother found them not to be accurate. Our baby didn't stay in one place. We were taking extra pre-cautions; although there were times that I had to remind my boyfriend to place the pillows when leaving the room.

He not only forgot to place the pillow, thinking he could make a quick trip to the refrigerator; he placed him too close to the edge of the bed in his hastiness.

I was hysterical. Although I was a nurse and was trying to do an assessment of him, I found it difficult to do so.

My mind immediately flashed back to a woman I knew whose baby had fallen out of his carrier and was taken to the emergency room, the same emergency room I would later take my son. Unfortunately, her son was sent back home and later he died. The thought of my son dying from a fall caused severe panic within me.

I had to pull myself together, calm myself down; I needed to take care of our baby. I looked at him. He had a circular abrasion on the side of his face and a small abrasion on his elbow. I checked his level of consciousness. He seemed to be fine. Although I observed no signs and symptoms of head trauma, from what I could assess through hysterics, I needed to be sure. We decided not to take any chances. We wanted to take him to the emergency room to be assessed and evalu-ated to make sure he was all right.

We took our son to the emergency room. The events that took place from that very moment of entering that hospital opened my eyes to what I had only heard about, read about, and this was where the nightmare escalated. We sat on each side of our son holding his tiny hands. I couldn't stop the tears. His father cried, blaming himself for being careless.

The doctor finally arrived and asked what had happened. He examined our baby, and then ordered a CAT scan, a computerized axial tomography to analyze the internal structure, to determine if our son had a skull fracture or other injuries resulting from trauma.

He also ordered a sedative prior to doing the scan. I felt somewhat uneasy with the medication he ordered to sedate him.

I was remembering my nursing training that certain medication should not be given if a head injury was suspected. One of the medicines he had ordered was Demerol, which could depress the respirations and has the capacity to elevate spinal fluid pressure in the presence of a head injury. He didn't know if our son had a head injury or not.

I had no idea who this doctor was; he did not know my son's medical history. My son had his own pediatrician, but no one cared to listen when I tried to tell them. They assumed I was another welfare case and automatically appointed a doctor for his care.

We followed the technician down to the area where the scan was to be performed. After it was completed, we waited for the results.

People began to act strange, but nothing ever crossed my mind. I was too concerned about my baby. Then, finally, we were told that they were going to keep him overnight for observation. I felt somewhat relieved, again thinking of the baby who was sent home and later died. I thought, at least he'll be here in the hospital just in case something goes wrong. If he does have any type of trauma, good observation was crucial, but little did I know that this was not the reason for his hospital stay.

I first found out when I heard one nurse say to the other, "This has already been done." She was pointing at something on the doctor's order. She didn't realize that I was also a nurse and could read doctor's orders. The order was to notify the health and rehabilitation service for child abuse.

If I hadn't been so upset because of my baby, I would have laughed at something so absurd. I would have taken it for a joke, but the nightmare ahead was far from a joke.

I was thankful to God that my baby didn't have a head injury, for more reasons than one. The fear of what could have happened overwhelmed me just thinking of the possible outcome resulting from all the sedatives he was given that were ordered by the doctor. Before my fears could be completely alleviated, he started to exhibit some side effects; side effects that were detrimental to us all, which would eventually affect his ability to respond, and leave him in an unarousable state, and would be evidence in the building of the child abuse case against his father and me.

Hospital

I WILL NEVER as long as I live forget the nightmare I experienced in that hospital from the very moment I entered until I exited. I had gained sixty- five pounds during my pregnancy. During the three or four days of my son's hospitalization, I had loss a great deal of that weight. I honestly don't remember eating a meal during the entire time I stayed with him. I simply had no desire to eat.

When I was told that my baby would be admitted in the hospital for observation, I was relieved knowing my baby would be in the hospital just in case he exhibited some problems later on.

I thought about the doctor who had examined my baby. He did so in a matter of minutes. He asked questions out of formality. He did not care for the answers we gave. He had determined that we were guilty of child abuse the moment he saw the bruise on my baby's face. This was the same doctor who ordered the computerized axial tomography scan.

My son was given Demerol, phenergan, and Thorazine. These drugs could have caused serious problems if my son had actually had a head injury. The combination of these medications has a delayed onset of action that last up to several hours and carry a risk of respiratory and cardiac arrest.

He was so drowsy, to the point where it was difficult to arouse him. I ended up crying countless tears as I held my near flaccid, sedated baby throughout the night following into the next day.

While in the emergency room, he had also received intramuscular injections, medication given via needle in his thigh muscle. He had blood drawn twice and was infused through an intravenous line to the right arm, which was splinted in place. Little did I know that everything that was done to him in the emergency room would later on set the stage and be used as evidence against us that child abuse actually existed. Our son was fine from the fall. All the medical intervention he was receiving had no association with the fall.

The medical staff talked among themselves as though I didn't exist. They had decided upon a pediatrician for my son; after all, I was already stereotyped and was treated as an illiterate single black woman, so they just assumed that I was just another welfare case, someone with no health insurance who had sought free medical attention from the clinic. In fact, this was later addressed in court. No one even made an effort to ask if I had a pediatrician. When I followed my son upstairs to his assigned room, I politely asked a nurse if she would call my son's pediatrician.

My son's father and I both shed tears for all that our son was going through. The only thing we could do at this point was to watch and hold his limp body. I knew there was no way I could leave him. I stayed with him day and night. His father had to leave for work.

As I sat holding and rocking my baby, I was surprised to see two men enter the room, one being a police officer and the other a child protective services investigator, who would literally make my life a living hell.

The officer looked at my baby, asked what had happened. He had me to write out a statement. He finished his investigation and left.

Later I read his "incident report" which was the beginning of the many discrepancies I would encounter. He wrote, *"I entered the room and observed an infant a little more than a month. I immediately noticed a large abrasion and bruising on the left cheek. This area was covering almost the entire side of the face."* Then he went on to say that, *"the investigator also pointed out bruises on the right leg both above and below the kneecap, on both arms and in the chest area. The bruises were indicative of rough handling, possibly pinching and poking. The bruise on the face resembles knuckles, possibly the back of a hand, also some sort of bruising on the forehead above his right eyes, between his brow and hairline."*

It finally began to dawn on me that these people were serious; they actually believed we abused our son.

I was more than happy to see my son's pediatrician enter the room. He had examined my baby four days prior at his office and gave him a complete physical. He examined him in the nude from head to toe.

I sat and watched as he again thoroughly examined my baby with a nurse by his side. I heard him ask the question, "Where are all the bruises over the baby's body?" Apparently, he had read the accusations. In his final report, he wrote, *"There is a bruised area over the left cheek, size of a quarter, and upper part of it shows a slight abrasion noted below the left eye. There is a small bruised area on the left elbow, which is the size of a dime. There are no other signs of trauma or any abrasion or bruises over the body."*

It was a relief to know that someone finally believed that my son was not abused, that the bruised area on the left side of the cheek and left elbow was consistent with his falling off the left side of the bed. I thought finally it was all settled. After all, this was his pediatrician, and he had something to compare. He had examined my baby previously.

But unfortunately his opinion wasn't good enough. Another report followed from the investigator, the man who determined to destroy my life. At the time, I didn't know the reason why.

He wrote an extensive report that left me speechless. I read some of the report, then I couldn't bear to read anymore. He wrote; "*The child has bruises on the left side of his head; a CAT scan is suspicious for a skull fracture, also the child was found to have a large bruise area on the left side of the face, below the eye and up into the eye. The area bruised was approximately the size and shape of an adult male hand. Also found were numerous bruises in various stages of healing on different areas of the body as follows; a dime size bruise to the right rib cage just below and to the left of the left breast, a two inch by half inch bruise on the outside of the upper left forearm just below the elbow, a dime size bruise on the belly to the right and above the navel, several small bruises above and below the right knee, a scrape and bruise on the inside of the left elbow, bruise on the front left shoulder at the armpit, and a quarter inch by one eighth inch cut on the upper right forehead.*"

At this point, I was beginning to get nervous. I realized this was beginning to get even more serious. Three reports were written on my son concerning his physical examination on the twenty-second day of July by three different people. Not anyone reading the reports would ever have believed they were speaking of the same baby.

My son advanced from a baby with minor injuries to a severely injured baby within a twenty-four hour period according to records, records that would be used to alter my mental status, which would leave my mind in turmoil.

I couldn't believe these experts in the field of law, who had so much power, control over my life at this time and so many others who had travelled this same path were describing punctured sites from needles during blood draws, intravenous line and intra-muscular injection sites as injuries resulting from child abuse.

Now the tears I shed were for not only the sorrow I felt knowing what my baby was going through, but also the thought of being accused of abusing him.

These people had no idea of the love, the bond I had for and with this child. If the thought of abusing him had ever crossed my mind, I would have taken it upon myself to seek help without hesitation and definitely would never have allowed anyone to abuse him.

I was still somewhat in the dark not knowing what was going on. The following day the HRS investigator again approached us.

I suppose at this time I had calmed down enough to see clearly through tear-dried eyes to observe the man who stood before us. He was a big, tall man with a Southern air about him. My psyche was beginning to work again. I immediately felt uneasiness about this man.

He held much of the conversation with my son's father. Although he portrayed himself to be friendly, kind and concerned, I knew it was all a facade.

He told him since he was the only one there with our baby when the incident occurred, that *he* would need to go to the courthouse to fill out paperwork and file a report, and told me that I didn't have to go. He acted as though it was not that important.

We somewhat relaxed, thinking everything was finally getting resolved. When my son's father got ready to leave, for some strange reason I decided to go with him. Although I hated to leave my baby's side, I wanted to know what was going on.

When we got to the courthouse, we had no idea where to go. We were instructed to go upstairs. When we reached our destination, we were surprised to see the HRS investigator along with other HRS officials. The investigator proceeded to hand us both papers. I couldn't believe what my eyes were seeing, what my mind was reading. We were accused of child abuse; our baby was going to be taken away from us and be placed in a foster home. I was almost in a state of shock. As I continued to read through blurred vision, I experienced the first sign that something was wrong.

First of all, the investigator had told me I didn't need to come to the court house; I had come here on my own. Now I was holding court orders stating I was also supposed to be present. I realized then he was trying to make me miss the court date.

The investigator went on to say that we were told to get a lawyer. He never mentioned anything about a lawyer to us. We didn't know until now why we were here, then he continued on saying we didn't have family to place the child with, now it was more than I could bear. I probably had the largest, closest knit family in the county.

The information he had typed was basically false information. I was suddenly afraid, because now I realized this was real.

I didn't know what to do nor who to call; I just couldn't burden my mother. I didn't want to upset her. The only person I could think of at that moment to call was my baby's pediatrician. After all, he had examined my baby; he knew he was not abused. I called him hysterically. I could hear my words echoing in my ears, "They are trying to take my baby away from me." He said to me, "They are not going to take your baby." With that assurance, I felt somewhat relieved.

We entered the courtroom without a lawyer. We were defenseless, and there stood across from us was the HRS lawyer and other HRS representatives. We stood and listened as they accused us as child abusers, as they requested our baby be removed from our home. There was nothing we could say or do. The judge granted their request and suggested we get a lawyer. I cried countless tears; all I wanted was to get back to the hospital to be with my baby. I hadn't involved my family because I had no idea it would come to this extreme.

A nurse at the hospital notified my family. I vaguely remember my family being there. I was so engulfed with grief; all I could think about was my baby being taken away. I wish I could have grabbed him and run with him, but I knew it would only make matters worse.

I had no desire to neither eat nor sleep. I waited, just as the death row inmates wait for someone to take them to have their life taken away, for kidnappers to take my baby. All of a sudden, I could relate to them. I was waiting for my life to be taken away. I just couldn't imagine living without him; I had to touch him, I needed to feel his chest rise and fall just to know that he was breathing. I had to bathe him, brush his hair, talk to him.

It was getting late in the evening. Perhaps somewhere in my cluttered mind there was hope that they wouldn't come. My hope was shattered as the big, tall, cold- hearted man entered the room to take my baby away.

I remember a nurse asking if I wanted to say goodbye. I

didn't want to say goodbye. Goodbye sounded so permanent. I wanted to scream, but I was too weak. The only sound I could make was the little moans that come from a broken heart. A nurse took me out of the room so I wouldn't see my baby being taken away. I was so stricken with grief until I could barely walk. She held me up and cried with me. I could never find the words to express the way I felt. I felt as though a part of me died, and I wanted the other part to die, but at the same time, I knew I had to live, for my son.

The nightmare had only just begun. I was told my son would be transferred to another hospital to be evaluated by experts, and they would determine if my son had been abused. Little did I know these so-called experts were part of the organization.

I don't know if they lied about their findings or if my son was truly in a battered state by the time he reached the hospital.

I don't think anyone could begin to imagine the pain of having a child taken away, knowing there's nothing that could be done nor said. What made it even worse was the fact that my son was taken at night. I never understood why; the hospital he was to be taken to wasn't more than an hour and a half away.

I was not only stricken with grief, but fear as well. All kinds of thoughts entered my mind. I was afraid this man would get in an accident traveling with my baby. I didn't know if he had a car seat.

I wasn't aware at this time that I was dealing with a racist. If I had known, I probably would have lost my mind from worrying what he was possibly doing to my baby. I had no idea where my baby was. All I could do was cry. I began to make phone calls once I arrived home, trying to find out where my baby was. No one would provide me with any information. I needed to know that he was all right, that he was safe.

Finally, someone decided to talk to me over the phone. He treated me like a criminal. His tone and words were as cold as ice. This man had no idea who I was. He immediately judged me. He heard one side of the story and based his opinion on what he had heard. That's all he was interested in, and he didn't care to hear my side. When I asked if he knew where my baby was, he said in the most hateful voice one can imagine, "You abused your baby, so you just have to wait." I suppose he said until tomorrow or wait until someone else tells me, I wasn't sure; I was too devastated to comprehend.

I remember calling my director, my employer. I figured she would have some kind of influence. I actually was not aware of what I was doing, but realized now I would need all the help I could get. This was too much of a battle for me. She was able to get some information. My baby wasn't taken to the hospital that night as I was told, but was instead placed in foster care, in a strange place with strange people. The countless tears started to flow again. Now I was beyond devastated. From the day my son was born, I had been so particular, so much in control of his care, and now all of this was loss. The sadness and fear was indescribable, I felt as though my baby had been kidnapped.

Public Defender

THINGS WERE MOVING so fast we didn't have time to prepare for anything. Sometimes I wonder if this wasn't part of the plan. All of this was so new to us, we didn't know which direction to turn, then finally a decision was made for us. A public defender was appointed to our case.

I think back on the day we were to appear in court with our appointed lawyer. He met with us approximately fifteen minutes prior to the time we were to appear. I'll never forget how we sat there while he occupied himself with whatever he was working on, barely making eye contact with us. When he finally finished, he hurriedly tried to gather information for the few minutes we had remaining before court.

One question and comment he made that I never forgot was, "Why did you all take your baby to the emergency room? I don't take my kids to the hospital when they fall." He was saying, when his children fall and bruise themselves, he doesn't take them to the hospital for fear of being accused of child abuse. This remark somewhat startled me.

Regardless of the pain of what I was going through, I couldn't imagine myself doing anything differently. If I had to do it all again, no way would I not have taken my son to the emergency room not knowing if he was injured or not.

I knew at this point, and it became even more obvious from other questions he asked, that this man was only doing the job he was appointed to do and nothing more. He had neither concern nor interest in ruling in our favor.

I was right in my judgment. When we entered the courtroom, this appointed lawyer just went through the motions. He made no effort to fight on our behalf, and he basically presented himself with us in the courtroom because this was a legal requirement. I think even if the interest was there, it wouldn't have made a difference. After all, how is it possible to effectively represent a client when there's no lawyer-client relationship, communication? He knew nothing about us and met us for the first time minutes before entering the courtroom, I doubt if he even knew our names without looking at the paperwork.

After walking out of the courtroom with negative results, I knew if this lawyer continued to represent us, I could risk losing my son for a long time if not forever. I knew I had to search for another lawyer, and time was crucial.

Dream

THE ELDERLY FOLK had a saying that when a person was able to "see things," or more like have a vision, that they were born with what they called a veil over their face.

I don't know about a veil or if there was any truth to it at all, but I do know throughout my life, mostly my adult life, I had experienced what some may call psychic experiences, premonitions, or perhaps just guardian angels watching over me.

These visions would occur by way of dreams. At times, I would be afraid to sleep, actually afraid of what I might dream.

Although I had experienced some unpleasant dreams or perhaps dreams that left me puzzled, fearful, and uncertain, the dreams I experienced during the time my son was taken was a message on my behalf.

In the dream, I saw this HRS worker, the man who would play the major role in my nightmare, though I didn't know it at the time. It was as though he was evil, the way he looked, the way he spoke. He said to me, "I have the power to destroy you," then I saw a name, as though it was engraved on a pocket where one would wear a nametag, a first and last name.

I woke up with mixed emotions. I had no idea what the

dream meant or if it meant anything at all. It was only a matter of days before the interpretation of the dream became a reality and would be the focus of my nightmare.

When I encountered the HRS investigator, it wasn't long before I realized that he was indeed the man in the dream.

The spoken words from the man in the dream were being put into action. He was certainly using whatever power he had to try to destroy me. I was well on my way to being destroyed physically, mentally, and financially.

I was almost too mentally drained to be as shocked as I normally would have been under different circumstances about the other puzzling part of the dream, the name I saw. I was trying so hard to find a lawyer, to get rid of the public defender assigned to our case, because of his lack of interest, just someone fulfilling an obligation. Since I had never had any involvement or a need for a lawyer, I was at a total loss. I had tried to call around, but got nowhere fast. Then I got a phone call one day, from a lawyer. When the lawyer introduced herself, it was unbelievable; it was the same name I had seen engraved on the pocket in the dream. I had no idea how she had gotten my phone number.

I had this one and only contact with her. She said to me that they wouldn't let her take my case; I believe it had something to do with the county I was living in. I wasn't even sure who she meant when she said they. I was too mentally exhausted to process information at the time and still somewhat in disbelief, but I do remember her giving me advice, telling me to be careful about the lawyer I choose. She told me to make sure he/she knows about HRS laws. To this day, I never knew who this lawyer was or where she was calling from, but she led me on the right path.

I got busy after this encounter searching for a lawyer

suitable for the case, remembering the mysterious person's advice. Also, I knew our case would end up with negative results if the public defender had continued to represent us.

Lawyer

THE DOCTOR I worked with recommended our lawyer. She had been the attorney for a well-known case. It was difficult trying to contact her, and I wasn't sure once I contacted her if she would even take the case. I tried calling, but was never able to talk with her, so I decided to write her a letter.

One day I received a call from her office for an appointment for us to meet with her. She told us she would take the case and reveal to me that she decided to do so after reading my letter that touched her heart.

We found out that she had been an HRS lawyer. Just hearing the word started to stir up doubt, making me wonder if I could truly trust her. What an awful feeling it was to lose trust, to be so fearful. I decided to take a chance. I knew I had to trust someone and, besides, I didn't feel threatened by her from the moment I met her. She presented herself to be a caring and compassionate person.

Once she took the case, I could immediately see the difference with her work, her effort, than that of the public defender. As I had heard many times, "You get what you pay for in life," and though it was getting quite expensive because of the fact that the case went on for months, it was worth all the sacrifices.

At one point during the case, our lawyer notified us that she could no longer represent us both. It was by letter. We were constantly receiving letters from the lawyer or the organization. I always dreaded opening them, fear of its negative contents; not many were positive. She wrote that she had received the discovery response from the Department of Health and Rehabilitative Services. She went on to say that when she had initially approached us, she was under the impression that our positions were identical and could represent us jointly without a problem, but after reviewing the documents produced by the HRS, she had come to the conclusion that she couldn't represent us both .

We had no idea what she was talking about. We were at a loss. Was the issue with him or me? We nervously met her at her office. She told us of the decision and why she made it. She was going to represent me only.

There was new so-called evidence of violence against my son's father, "killing a cat by smashing his head against a wall." She had actually received information that he was seen doing so.

Because of such, the case now took another turn, had become more difficult, too much for her to focus on while trying to reunite me with my son. Therefore, the decision was made to represent me only, because such an accusation would have bearing on the case that could possibly result in my not getting my son back, and reuniting me with my son was priority. HRS was still working from every angle.

My son's father understood her decision to represent me, so now we started separate cases; he was directed to seek another attorney.

My lawyer fought long and hard, and it was getting more and more expensive as time passed, which was somewhat scary for me. I just couldn't let finances be the obstacle in preventing me from getting my son back. Whatever the cost, even if it meant me working two or three jobs, I was willing to pay the price to get my son back. Fortunately, as the case went on, my attorney realized it was racially based and decided that she would no longer charge any more money. She said this was her way of paying back what society had done to us.

The Devil in Disguise

I ALWAYS SAID I was given another gift, to vibe a person. It's as if I can "feel" that person, perhaps something similar to what people experience when they talk about chemistry between them. Mine, however, detects the negative and the positive.

When the child protective investigator walked into the hospital room, the feeling wasn't pleasant. Even though he tried to portray himself as a kind, caring, and concerned person, I knew I felt he wasn't genuine. Something was wrong. I knew I had to be careful. I had to observe him; I had to listen closely. Because of everything I was experiencing, I was vulnerable, and my state of mind had been traumatized.

Even after he had written his original report documenting the bruised areas he found over my baby's body, and though he exaggerated, a part of me wanted to believe he made a mistake in his findings, or that he didn't have enough medical knowledge to differentiate bruises resulting from abuse from those resulting from medical procedures.

I refused to accept the fact that he was doing this intentionally. It was confirmed. I could see a pattern forming. I could no longer try to rationalize his behavior. I had to face the realization that my suspicion was right.

After a series of events, it wasn't long before I realized this man had a plan. He was out to destroy me and felt he had the power to do so. I think at first he felt as though he didn't need to put forth too much effort. After all, through his eyes I was just an uneducated, black woman with minor intelligence. It wasn't until later that he found out that I was quite the opposite, with the exception that I was indeed a black woman, but far from ignorant, so therefore he had to use stronger tactics, but unfortunately, his evils strengthened as well.

I was astounded when I read the investigator report. It was written in black and white, didn't take a trained eye to see what this man had set out to do. It was impossible for any professionals not to recognize such. There was so much negative, so many discrepancies, and so many lies. He had written it to justify his accusations of child abuse, to build his case, in hope that it would result in our punishment. He tried every approach.

In one of his beginning statements, he wrote I didn't want to take my baby to the hospital for fear of HRS getting involved in the case. HRS never crossed my mind. My only concern was my baby's well-being. Never would I have jeopardized my baby's life because of fear of HRS. Even if he had actually been abused, I still would have taken him and risked him being taken rather than him possibly losing his life.

This man had no idea as to the person I was. If I had abused my baby, I would have sought help and would have welcomed the intervention. The same applied if I had allowed anyone else to do so, which was included in another part of the report. He wrote, "The child is still considered to be at high risk for abuse due to the mother's previous failure to protect him from the ongoing abuse by the father and her inability to protect him in the home without services in place."

Again, I was almost speechless after reading this. This

was false information he was presenting before the court. The stereotype was taking place again, classing me with other women who allowed such in their relationship. This man had no knowledge about my family background, the importance of family that would never have allowed me to sit back, observe my baby being abused, and not take actions.

I had come from a strong family, a family whose classification didn't fit any of their categories. Through struggling to survive, it left us with such a unique family bond, one that was/is unbreakable. This was beyond absurd. Then I had to stop and think, this man had no interest in who I was nor the truth. This was his intention. This was what he needed to build his case. He was now on a roll. Next he wrote, "The couple was not accepted by his or her parents." Not sure how this fitted into his puzzle of deceit. My guess is this was to be one of the stressors that contributed to the allege abuse.

The truth was my son's father had a good relationship with my mother and the rest of my family and was accepted easily. Again, this man didn't know the uniqueness of my family. Even though my mother had her share and experienced much prejudice throughout her life, she never taught us prejudice and hate. What she taught us was that we should love one another. Therefore, it wasn't an issue when a relative wanted to bring someone of another race to family gatherings or whatever the occasion. They were always welcomed with open arms.

As far as my son's paternal grandmother, I don't know if it was a matter of acceptance or as it was, in her words, "wasn't expecting her son to date a black woman." The fact of the matter was, rather accepted or not, I wasn't looking for acceptance and didn't devote time or effort focusing on such. This indeed was not an issue. I didn't live and still today don't

live my life worrying if someone accepts me or likes me, because, after all, the problem lies within those who utilize their
energy and waste life harboring hate and dislike. I just ask that
respect is shown toward me, and this is all I expected from
his mother.

If the investigator had allowed me to elaborate, I would
have informed him that this indeed was not a stress factor in
my life.

As I continued to read the investigator's report, one comment stuck in my mind. In an effort to add onto my other
negatives to justify even further my potential to be a child
abuser, he wrote that I had no active involvement in any
church- related or civil activities.

I was raised in a religious household. No alcohol, drugs,
smoking, profanity; we had a peaceful household. I had attended church all of my life with the Sunday meals afterward.

What he had written made me wonder, had I never attended church in my life, and for the people who don't attend
church, does it make them "bad" people? Does it make me a
bad person? Does it lay out the blueprint? Is one destined to
be a child abuser because he or she isn't involved in certain
activities?

His tactics were beginning to weigh on my mind, but I
had to stop and realize the reason was just to introduce another negative approach. I can imagine him saying, *if nothing
else influenced them, this will*. After all, much of society, especially people in the good ole South, frown upon non-church
goers and label them as immoral people with little or no values at all.

Although my heart was heavy dealing with this nightmare,
and making it through another day took all the energy I willed
myself to have, my heart and thoughts went out to others who

had experienced similar situations. People were being judged and labeled because of their upbringing, educational background, religious beliefs, marital status, race, and the list goes on.

A biblical quote states, "A man looketh on the outward appearance, but God looketh on the heart." I had to retrieve the words my mother implanted into my mind when I needed consoling, when I needed a peace of mind. She would say to us, "It is a good thing that God is not like man." It is a consolation in knowing that he is the true judge.

I watched and listened in disbelief at this man who stared us in the face and lied. As we stood baffled in the courthouse, I had no idea that this would be only the beginning of the many lies to come, and the man who stood before us was the devil in disguise.

After my baby was taken, we had to meet with the investigator at his office. I remember walking into his office, and as I opened the door I was unpleasantly greeted by a large rebel flag covering a great portion of the wall in this state building. He made it quite obvious that it had nothing to do with pride, but prejudice.

In conversation, it wasn't long before he addressed and made comments about my biracial baby, not being black nor white, as though he didn't have an identity. I stared at him, thinking about his remark and the many others who make such an ignorant statement. What did he mean, and why was it of any importance that my baby wasn't black nor white? I honestly don't remember if I said to him or to myself that he was correct, he wasn't black or white; he was both.

Immediately I again started to recognize that something wasn't quite right. I was here to get to the truth, to get my baby back home, and this man was focusing on the race of my child. It was time for the punishment to begin. It was also quite obvious from his further comments and conversation that he didn't like the mixing of the races, and we were going to pay dearly.

His first approach was to get my son's father to turn against me, a tactic he thought for certain would be effective. He was unsuccessful because there was nothing to compromise. No crime had been committed. We had nothing to hide.

Since I, in his eyes, had been the one who "contaminated" the race, he thought I deserved the most punishment, so his goal was to destroy me in whatever way necessary.

My son's father told of how he questioned him about me, trying to get him to admit that I had taken drugs. He informed him that I was so health conscious that I didn't even drink soda, not to mention the fact that I didn't know what alcohol tasted like. It was almost comical to him just the thought of this investigator suggesting I used drugs. He refused to accept and be a part of his scheme.

Since the investigator's approach failed, and he couldn't get a confession, he decided to take another approach; he would use my baby's movement--the same movement that had been said previously wasn't possible for a baby his age, according to textbooks, describing what babies should be doing at what age. Though as the years passed, more and more is being recognized that one baby does not fit all; what applies to one doesn't necessarily apply to another. I knew what my baby was capable of doing. Now he wanted the movement to be used as evidence, as proof that my using drugs was what caused my baby movement.

Thank goodness for my gynecologist, who intervened and testified on my behalf that I had not used drugs. He had been my gynecologist for years and had monitored me closely from the time my pregnancy was confirmed to delivery and knew the struggle I went through for my baby and my survival. In fact, he found such accusations upsetting, knowing all that I had been through with my pregnancy, all the medical issues, and my trying so hard to do everything right for the sake of my child.

When it was becoming obvious that race was indeed an issue in my case, HRS officials tried to defend the investigator by contacting the media with information on his behalf, stating he had a Masters degree in criminology and had moved to this county after asking for a transfer two years prior and that he had received excellent work reviews.

I remember vaguely being at work one day when the news reporters arrived. They interviewed me and talked about the investigator, stating someone had done a background check on him. Apparently, he was in law enforcement in the Deep South and had some type of confrontation with a black man that ended tragically, so there was a reason for his transfer.

Because one has a degree does not eliminate him from prejudice. Actually, people in this category are the most dangerous ones, the so- called intelligent minds, who hide behind education just like the "modern day Klans." Once Klansmen were thought to be ignorant, uneducated people, until the new klans were formed with educated leaders, public speakers able to change and rearrange their vocabulary. Regardless of how words are structured,the definition remains the same,not many words replace hate,prejudice,racism; these educated leaders just present them in a more *intellectual* way.

The investigator just had an upper hand. He was educated and in a position where he could inconspicuously work without the hood. His evil continued throughout the trial, but slowly his disguise would be revealed.

Adoption

DURING THIS ORDEAL, I researched and gathered any information I thought would be beneficial. Somewhere in the process, I received a book that described the HRS as the witch-hunt. The book provided some disturbing information. The stories told were from actual cases and results from research that had been done. Although the book was informative, I was somewhat devastated and left with the feeling of doom. At one point in my life it would have been difficult to believe what I was reading, but now, with all that I had experienced, not only did I believe, I knew the possibilities.

When I read how the organization had taken children away from their parents and actually put them up for adoption, a feeling overwhelmed me, something I couldn't express in words. According to the book, they didn't need necessary facts. In some cases, there was no evidence that these parents were unfit or had abused their children, yet their children were still put up for adoption. Then it went on to say that there were other cases where children were put up for adoption because of the demand, especially white male babies. Many couples were waiting for the opportunity to adopt a male child. My situation could have been another chapter in the book. All of a sudden, I was afraid like never before.

I will never forget the anonymous phone call I received one morning. I had no idea at the time who the caller was, but I would find out later on and call her my guardian angel. The caller said to me in a panicky tone, *"You have to do something in a hurry. They are talking about taking your baby away from you and putting him up for adoption."* I was almost speechless with an indescribable sickness in my stomach. I simply could not believe what I was hearing. It was difficult to believe that these people would go to such extremes, but then I started to think of all the unjust things they had done thus far and realized they were capable of doing anything.

I started to remember what I had read in that book, children taken, given to couples to adopt. Although I should have gotten some release by knowing the book spoke of white male babies, I didn't because my son could have easily passed for white. In fact, all of his hospital records described him as a white male, so instead I panicked even more.

I couldn't understand how easily these people could take a child away from the parents and just give him/her to someone else as though the child was a domestic animal, with no regard to the bond between that of the child and the parents. Now I knew without a doubt that this case was unusual. We were never officially charged with child abuse because there was no evidence, regardless of the efforts to try to present any, yet they were talking about taking my son away from me.

There was no way I was going to let this happen. I had to fight harder than ever. Just the thought of the possibility of my son being put up for adoption literally made me sick. Now I had more than that strange feeling in my stomach. I could barely eat.

I had already lost significant weight. Had it not been for all the extra weight I had gained during my pregnancy, I'm not sure I would have survived losing that much of my normal weight unplanned and at such an accelerated rate. This was unhealthy and was draining me mentally and physically.

I knew I had to gain control. If I was unable to take care of my son because of being in such state, it would only give them another reason to justify why my son should be put up for adoption.

Guardian Angel

I HAD ALWAYS been the type of person who had treated people fairly and with respect. I believe in the saying "What goes around, comes around."

Just when I thought my world was falling apart, it was as though the good Lord intervened. Different things started happening. I knew God had not forsaken me. I remember a letter that I had written to my attorney telling her basically how God prepared me ahead of time. It was like whatever evil, meaning the dishonesty, deceitfulness, the wrongdoing, slandering that was bestowed upon me, I was always one-step ahead. I Remembered when it all started, my showing up at the courthouse when the investigator told me I didn't need to be there, yet I felt an urge to go anyway.

It didn't matter how others portrayed me, I knew the relationship I had with God. Although at some point I lost hope, only because the situation was becoming overwhelming, too much to bear. It started affecting me mentally as well as physically. I was almost losing my strength to fight. Little did I know the good Lord was touching someone else's heart and mind. I called her my guardian angel. She was the voice on the other end of the phone call I received, warning me that I had to do something because they were trying to take my baby from me.

I finally got to meet the woman whose voice was on the other end of the phone, a pleasant woman who was also a Christian. She was an HRS worker. The woman wasn't initially involved in the case, and she had been on vacation, but had apparently heard about the case.

I remember her saying sometime during the case that she was in bed, got up, read her bible, then said to herself, "There is something wrong with this case." She started to look into the case and from the very beginning realized this case was handled differently from the many other cases. There were many discrepancies concerning the case. This was a comment she made to the media. She refused to take part in any wrongdoing.

According to court records and newspaper articles, she approached the investigator when she found out my baby had been placed in foster care rather than with relatives and asked why he hadn't followed policies and procedures of placing the baby with relatives.

The investigator told the caseworker to cease her investigation because he needed to "build a case" against us and told her at the time that she shouldn't be supportive of us because it was a "white man living off a Black woman." He thought he would try this approach to turn her against the white man since she, too, was black, and by doing so, it would destroy me as well.

He was determined to punish us for crossing the color barrier. She refused to give in to his scheme. Instead, she continued to research the case, but in doing so, she became a target. She had worked for the organization for many years. Suddenly, her job was threatened. She herself had to hire a lawyer for her own defense.

She testified on my behalf. She told of how the case was

handled differently from the many other cases, how she had walked into a staff meeting and other staff, along with the investigator, found great humor and laughed about the incompetent public defender appointed to my case, knowing they had nothing to worry about. What they were not aware of was the fact that I had hired a new lawyer, a well-known one.

The caseworker stated when she mentioned to them the name of the attorney I hired, they immediately started to review and change documents. The caseworker said at the deposition that, before her arrival, all papers were taken from her concerning my case, but she memorized dates and what was written.

I will never forget the sacrifice this woman made for me, a total stranger; she jeopardized her job of many years. I realize that she was only doing what was right, but, like me, she was lied to, accused and ridiculed, but through it all she held on to the truth and her faith, and she did prevail in the end. She knew the truth would set her free. It was a lesson to learn for me, to continue to fight, hold on to my faith, and wait for this same truth to set me free.

The Judge

FOR MANY PEOPLE, the South was synonymous with prejudice. I had heard stories, but in my mind, I placed them in a different era, perhaps because I didn't want to believe that such hatred and evil actually existed in what was to be a land of freedom, a land of equality. Here we were, advancing in technology, brilliant minds being used, yet some brilliant minds were filled with prejudice. These were dangerous minds because they belonged to those who had position and power. This combination allowed one to destroy, to make unethical decisions with no repercussions.

I was left without a choice to bring the real South back into reality as I listened to a co-worker one night at work. The young man hadn't been employed at this establishment for long, he was a kind and caring person.

One night as we sat down to eat, he started to talk. At that moment, from his conversation, I realized that he was overly qualified for the position he held. He had worked in the court system close to the judges, yet he had taken a position with much less pay and prestige. Before that night was over, I knew the reason why.

He began to talk about things that happened and things he had heard, the reason he could no longer work in that type of environment. He left also with a guilty conscience and was in a dilemma. He said he actually heard confessions of crimes, committed by the judges who were not only his boss, but people with great power, so who was he to report to?

He told of how they used racial slurs in the chamber, the unfair sentencing. The story he told that topped them all was about one of the judges, who was well known to many in the community, who laughed and bragged about a crime he had committed in his past and how he had gotten away with it. The worker said the crime the judge spoke of was murder. He said he listened as the judge confessed in a humorous manner that he set fire to a black man, which resulted in his death.

The mistake that many people make is assuming that because a person is of the same race, whether black, white or whatever nationality, that they have the same views. This reminds me of a patient's complaint about a dentist who was working on his teeth and making racial remarks about black people. The man was white, but his wife was black.

I had no idea that I, too, would encounter one of those minds with the position, power, and prejudice. As laws changed and people began to utilize their civil rights, racism took a more subtle change. Unbeknownst to me, the presiding judge who handled my case was from the town I had graduated high school from eighteen years prior, the town that had opposed integration of school among other things, and the town where the disaster happened with the case of the four black men and white woman.

When I walked into the courtroom to face the judge, I was engulfed by that feeling that was now well known to me, that bad vibe. My first appearance before him was without legal representation. It was basically a set-up. My son's father and I were totally unprepared. We had no forewarning. Not only did we not have any idea that we had to appear before a judge, we didn't know the reason why, so we were on our own.

The Judge acted as though we were invisible in the court-room, totaling ignoring us. I watched as he gave his undivided attention to the HRS lawyer and people of the organization, listening closely at the accusations, to their request, which was to take our baby away, to place him in a shelter. He granted it without hesitation, not acknowledging us at all. Throughout the case, he presented the same type of attitude.

Another time in the courtroom, I thought it was odd that he would get so involved as far as his voicing his opinion instead of listening to the evidence and other information presented before him. He was providing information to help build a case and information that was detrimental to my case. I remember him suggesting to the accuser that the bruise on my son's cheek could have possibly been made by a ring on a male's finger. It was just the way he said it that led me to believe he, too, was trying to assist in building a case against us. It was agreed upon that this was, indeed, a ring print, that it occurred when my son's father hit him. I never had the op-portunity to say it could not be true, because his father had never worn a ring.

I believe in giving a person the benefit of the doubt. I suppose in the case of the Judge, I didn't want to believe that this man, who basically had so many people's lives in his hand, who basically determined the outcome of a person's life, would be tainted by prejudice. Even though this was his personal right, I wanted to believe and trust that he would make ethical, moral decisions based on facts, and while in the power seat, rule beyond his prejudice.

At one point, I doubted myself and thought perhaps he was just doing his job, but again my suspicion was confirmed.

A woman who got involved in my case worked in the court system and knew the Judge. After assessing the situation, realizing who I was as a person, and from her expertise realizing there was no abuse, trusted me enough to reveal something that could have no doubt gotten her into some serious trouble. I think also she felt as though she was doing the right thing, perhaps to give me a warning.

She, in so many selective words to protect herself as well, told me the Judge was a racist. She told me about an incident that had happened concerning an interracial couple whom she knew. They had sat in a restaurant near where the judge and his guests were dining. The judge intentionally talked in a loud enough voice for the couple to hear about interracial relationships and how he opposed them.

She didn't get into the rest of the conversation. She gave me enough information to make me aware of what was really happening. I think she wanted me to be ahead of the game, to be prepared for what was in store for me.

Psychologist I

I REMEMBER AN HRS worker telling me not to go to the Psychologist assigned by the HRS for the psychological evaluation because she was "working along with them." I didn't understand what she meant by this. It didn't make sense to me and sounded like something that happens in a movie. I thought truly nothing like this exists in real life. Besides, this woman was a professional. Then for a moment the thought did occur to me, the way things were going, this could be possible. After all, many of the people I was dealing with are professionals. Then I refused to think that a woman of her stature would jeopardize her career to indulge in such deceit.

I was far from wrong. It wasn't long after I took a seat in her isolated office when she began to question me before I started to realize the worker had been right in her judgment of this woman. Much as she tried to project a professional attitude, it was quite obvious that the true woman behind the mask was putting me back into that stereotype line; a woman who was incapable of controlling her emotions, a woman who wasn't professional enough to not let her personal feelings and opinion get involved into her work.

She started immediately talking to me in a way I was coming very familiar with as if I were another "uneducated black woman." Two questions she asked remained in my mind for a long time.

At that moment, when she asked the questions, I was drained emotionally. I didn't have the energy to respond in the manner that I've thought so many times afterward that I should have. Under different circumstances, I don't think that I would have sat there and let this woman belittle me, nor would I have tried to explain to her or try to justify why I did the things that I did. Who was she to judge me as if she was God?

Unfortunately, I wasn't in control of my situation. All I could think about was getting my baby back. I just wanted the truth to be known that I wasn't insane nor had any type of psychological disorder.

One of the questions asked was, "Why did you decide to have a baby before you were married?" Before I could explain, which I shouldn't have had to do, she quickly voiced her opinion. "Most people wait until they are married to have a baby." This woman sat before me, a thirty-six- year- old woman, talking to me as if I were a child, lecturing me on society's expectations as if I were insane for having a child out of wedlock, as if I were the first person to ever do so. I had no regrets no matter what she nor society thought of me.

The next question shocked me. "Why do you date white men?" Again, she immediately made a connecting comment as she did the first question, "Because there is a shortage of Afro-American men?" I have yet to remember how I answered this question. I would have liked to have answered it by asking her if my dating white men was cause enough to diagnose me with a mental illness that would in return cause me to abuse my child. After all, this was my reason for being here, for this professional woman to determine my mental state, yet her concern was more about me dating outside my race. Words could not describe the way I felt.

I was listening to this woman and not believing what I was hearing in this day and time, in this century. Because I was attracted to someone of another race, something was wrong with me mentally. I found this to be frightening, not only for myself, but for the millions of people I shared this world with who have their own personal attractions, rather it be someone of another race, hair color, eye color, height, weight, or whatever the attraction may be. This type of mentality from the professionals, who many regard highly, and who are classed as experts, have no doubt led many sane people behind institutional walls and innocent people behind prison walls.

I noticed the switch in her questioning when she finally realized that I wasn't as ignorant as she thought. This came about only after she probed into my background and found out that I had done some extensive traveling within the states and other countries as well and had also *attended college in Germany*. I even had a degree in nursing, much to her surprise.

She then started to shift her questions, asking why I would date a man like my baby's father, meaning a man who was not equally educated. I just found it so surprising that this professional woman was so opinionated.

The saddest part of it all, regardless of her line of questioning, I was obligated to answer, because basically she had my life within her hands, meaning my son, who was my life. Based on her findings, it would be the determining factor if my son would be returned to me.

She finally asked questions that pertained to my baby's incident, but again questioning and voicing her opinion on what couldn't have happened and what did happen. She presented some photos given to her by the Child Protective Services representative. In the photo was a picture of my baby with his arm wrapped in gauze, the purpose, to keep the intravenous line in place. This woman refused to believe me when I told her the reason for the wrapping. She insisted that my baby's arm had been broken. Perhaps this was what was told to her. Later I knew it was all part of the building of the case.

I was amazed that this woman had spent such a short period of time with us, yet presented an extensive report, just as the investigator had done, diagnosing us with psychological disorders. Eventually it was revealed in court that she had spent less time with us to do a psychological evaluation than she had done any of her other clients.

From her strange line of questioning, she determined that I had a disorder based partially on the fact that I dated white men and the fact that I had a child out of wedlock.

This woman was considered an expert witness. I read in her report that I was a "fake good" a person who appears or is presented as being genuine, but is not. The only things she knew about me were what I told her in a short period of time. Was she that much of an expert that she could look at me, look back into my past, and say that everything that I had done for myself, for others, and the person that I am is a fake?

Again, I not only felt concern for myself, but I thought of the many others who had been falsely diagnosed and lives perhaps shattered as a result of it.

This so-called expert had gathered theorized information that she was presenting to the court that was far from the truth. I must admit that in a way she was somewhat of an expert because she truly had the ability to gather bits and pieces of information and present it in a way completely from its true meaning.

The reason for the referral to her was for the purpose of assessing our mental status and intelligence, to evaluate our capacity to adequately parent, and to determine if physical abuse potential existed. Of our psychological evaluation, of course, we were both diagnosed with a personality disorder. I was diagnosed with a dependent/compulsive disorder; he was diagnosed with a Compulsive disorder.

When I took out my psychology book to confirm the definition, for a moment I laughed, then I realized the sincerity of it all. Here this expert, according to the state, had diagnosed me with a disorder, one that would determine when and if I would get my baby back, that was completely the opposite of who I was. Anybody who knew me would have strongly disagreed with her findings. The book described the disorder as a person who lacks self-confidence and is unable to function in an independent role. It further read, "The person allows others to become responsible for him."

I had started my independent role as a teenager. Though my mother was always there for me, at a point in my life I felt that she had done so much that it was time for me to venture out, take responsibility of myself, and ease her load. I honestly don't remember ever asking my mother for another dollar from the time I started working in my teens until adulthood.

After high school, I travelled independently and eventually moved out on my own. I remembered traveling via a Greyhound bus at the age of eighteen, leaving my country town that didn't even have a traffic light. I headed to New Jersey by way of New York, destined to keep a promise that I had made to my mother to find her sister whom she hadn't seen for about forty years. I accomplished that mission.

Later on, I joined the military. Although I started my education toward my degree while in the military, I didn't complete it before discharge. Unfortunately, I was not able to get the GI Bill to use toward education; therefore, I worked and paid my way through college.

This woman didn't have a clue as to my independence. It wasn't bad enough that she labeled me with this disorder; she found words to define the disorder in such a negative way that it would leave the reader no choice but to see me as a potential psychotic child abuser. Her definition: *"Behind the front of propriety and restraint are intense rebellious feelings which are rarely exposed. In an effort to keep them constrained, the person often binds them so tightly that they themselves become over organized in an anxiety way. As a consequence of such constraint, similar persons are inclined to develop numerous and persistent psycho physiological symptoms."*

I noticed throughout her written evaluation she made it a point under each category; the behavior observations, the intellectual evaluation, the personality evaluation, and other evaluated areas-- to bring out a negative point to overrule the positive.

In the behavioral observation, she wrote that I was *"neatly dressed and groomed in a fashionable manner,"* then the next sentence read, *"Her fingernails were observed to be very long."*

I realized the purpose of this observation was to confirm that I had possibly been the one who had "dug my fingernails into my baby," as it had been previously stated.

She summarized the referral questions before giving her recommendations. She wrote that, although I was perceived to be a perfect mother, there were some drawbacks in my capacity to adequately parent my baby, that I was an over-anxious, rigid mother, maybe having problems adjusting to motherhood, that there were some elements of neglect surrounding my behavior in that I returned to my full-time job without having made adequate arrangements for the care of my infant whom I left for eight hours one day with a neighbor, and the following day with the baby's father.

Actually, his father had babysat him the first day. She documented him babysitting the day of the allege abuse. She also stated that his father had just been fired from a job. Had he been working, he would not have been available to watch our baby.

The preparation for motherhood started long before my baby was born, but no one wanted to hear the truth. Again, I was already stereotyped and a statistic. My unborn baby played a major role in motivating me to pursue my education. I was determined to provide a good life for my child without assistance from the state.

My education and hands on experience was also my preparation for motherhood. I read, observed, learned from the best, my mother, and had the opportunity to work with children all of my life. I had over seventy nieces and nephews. I had worked at a daycare. I had more than my share of experience.

Every time I read where this expert accused me of being an inadequate parent and of neglecting my baby, my head automatically moved from side to side in disbelief with words echoing in my mind "if she only knew." I could have taught the parenting class. I had books, brochures, videos, I watched the program "What Every Baby knows" and any other information I could gather concerning parenting.

Motherhood was a complete joy to me. I never dreaded a moment of getting up through the night to feed, change, or just to check him, and I looked forward to the mornings to bathe him, dress him, sing, and talk to him.

If this woman only knew just how organized I was. After all, I had spent years in the military; half- stepping was not part of my life. I wasn't the type to make a move without a plan. This so- called expert who knew little about me, only what I told her in a short period of time, presented information stating I returned to work without making arrangements for my son. Perhaps this was added just to again confirm that I really did have a disorder. Because, after all, one would have to be somewhat mentally disturbed to just up and go back to work, as in my case, without any thought of what to do with his/her child.

I had no time to think about my intelligence being insulted. It was enough just trying to prove that I was sane.

The truth is, the more I read and thought about what this psychologist had written, it left me wondering if she didn't have some type of disorder herself or if it was prejudice clouding her ability to be just and honest.

How could she diagnose me with a disorder that involved neglect because I left my baby with an adult neighbor well into her thirties whom I had known for almost four years? How many people leave their children with teenage babysitters?

I think what really floored me was when she wrote of my baby's father's incapability to adequately parent his baby. This was another reason she stated I was neglectful, because I left my son with his father, who didn't have any parenting education.

From these statements, it was becoming quite obvious that something was seriously wrong. This woman accused me of neglect because I had done what normal people do on an everyday basis. When did it become a crime to leave a child with a parent, and how many fathers in the United States, in the world, hadn't taken parenting classes prior to becoming parents? Because we were of a different race, did it make us different human beings? Were we supposed to abide by different laws? Did we not have the capability or the intelligence to raise children?

I think what was even more frightening than this expert psychologist was the fact that the HRS and the Judge actually saw this as neglect, and this was used against me. Of course again, I would understand why later.

I will never forget the horrible picture painted of us. Everything we said was used against us, no matter how positive. It was unfortunate that the Miranda rights didn't apply in this situation, the right to remain silent to avoid self-incrimination.

Whatever we said and didn't say was held against us in court. We had no rights. Not only were the positives turned into negatives, a simple statement was interpreted into something totally opposite from its meaning, leaving me baffled and astounded.

In her case dynamics she wrote, *"This couple was in the throes of a relationship conflict regarding marriage and their future when the infant's injuries occurred."* Never had we had a conflict about marriage.

It was something we had discussed, and we were no different from others who make plans or set goals before marriage. It was never an issue. We were satisfied with our relationship, and this again was to rationalize why we "injured our baby."

I mentioned to her how I would check on my baby throughout the night, look at him breathe, touch him. After all, is this not what mothers do? Is this not part of bonding, loving, caring? Well, for me, I was classed as an "over-anxious, rigid mother having problems adjusting to motherhood," so therefore, there were some elements of neglect surrounding my behavior.

Since stressors are the perfect indicator for child abuse, she wrote that there were several "additional" stressors present in our household at the time our baby was injured, such as the father's employment and my return to full-time employment.

What was so ironic is, others would probably have begged for the little stress we had in our lives. This expert, like the others in this triangle, just made assumptions, assuming he was stressed because he lost his job, not making it known that this job was not his major job. He was employed as a surveyor, but worked a part- time job to supplement his income. Of course, if she had, the painted picture wouldn't look so horrible.

Finances were never a problem. Financial arrangements were made prior to my son's birth. I was never in a financial bind, and as far as being stressed because I returned to my full-time job after "six weeks," *stressed* was a heavy word to use.

Like most mothers, I regretted leaving my son, but not stressed, and especially not so that I would abuse him.

After evaluating our stressors, she made her recommendations. "Since there is an unstable family situation in their household with poor management of stress, it is my opinion that their infant would be at risk if it were returned to them at this time."

We were heading down a one-way street, a dead end. Nothing that was said mattered. It was even written that my responses to the "child abuse inventory" produced an invalid profile because of a strong desire on my part to present myself only in positive terms, invalid because I spoke the truth. My honesty brought forth another disorder, "a fake-good response pattern," which suggested that I had serious problems in dealing with others.

I made another honest mistake of saying I tried to be a perfect mother, and others viewed me as such. Making such a remark caused her to add another disorder. She wrote, "Such a style of relating to others can be seriously problematic in that similar individuals are often very rigid in dealing with everyday issues and have difficulty with spontaneous and non-structured situations as is, of course, often found in child rearing." Reading this reminded me of the saying, "What does this have to do with the tea in China?"

Basically, the entire report was negative, another tool used to build a case against us. I had some doubts and disbelief when people spoke of people in position and prejudices.

I suppose I had lived so long in a state of denial. I just didn't want to believe that people in professional positions would allow racism and prejudice to cross over into their educated minds, clouding their ability to make ethical decisions. I suppose I've always equated racism and prejudice with ignorance, then ignorance with lack of education. Ignorance is defined as the lack of knowledge. However, what I've come to realize is, education doesn't exempt one from being ignorant, because though one may be knowledgeable in their specialty area or certain fields, they lack knowledge in other areas, mainly when dealing with the human race.

Here before me was an educated woman, but in a sense, she was ignorant; of course, this was just my evaluation of her.

The Caseworker

THE CASEWORKER ASSIGNED to my case was a woman perhaps in her mid- thirties or forties. The moment I set eyes on this woman, I knew something wasn't quite right with her. At the time I couldn't pinpoint it. She had a strange personality and acted as though her mental status wasn't up to par.

On one occasion, I was to have visitation with my son. By now all visits had to be arranged for his father and me, and usually separate, and when it was convenient for the caseworker. I waited for her to bring him to me. I waited and watched as the hours passed. She never arrived. I was not only disappointed, but was extremely worried. I had no idea where my baby was. I feared she had gotten in an accident. I waited in the rain; I was devastated, all kinds of thoughts entered my mind.

There was no consideration at all. No one called, nor was I able to call anyone to ask the whereabouts of my son or what had happened. I don't know how I survived the night or when the tears ever stopped.

I found out eventually that she had my son at her house. I wasn't sure if she was getting attached to him or if this was some type of cruel punishment. I didn't know what to think anymore. Neither she nor anyone else ever provided me with an explanation or an apology; I gather they figured an "abuser" didn't deserve either.

It was almost two months, and I was still fighting to be reunited with my son. This woman had to write a risk assessment for reunification. It was extremely negative, as though she was describing an entirely different person. This woman had no idea as to who I truly was. The person she described in the assessment, in layman's term, was a psychotic brutal unfit mother. She even referred back to the "psychological evaluation," stating I had a personality disorder with primarily dependent and compulsive features coupled with mild depression and went on to say that I might have difficulty with spontaneous situations as are needed in child rearing.

She also mentioned more times than one that I "failed to protect" my son, and although his father was gone, I would let him return. I suppose she was a mind reader as well. Needless to say, my overall risk assessment was rated "High," and I would continue my battle in court.

It's just strange or perhaps just coincidental how things happen. My sister was in line at a government building and overheard two women talking about this same caseworker. According to them, she was an alcoholic and was seen at the Alcoholic Anonymous meetings.

When I heard this, I immediately began to exhibit mixed emotions. I thought of all the times when she had driven my baby around with her and wondered if she was under the influence of alcohol during those times or perhaps if this was the reason she didn't show up for visitation. Again, my intuition had not forsaken me. I knew from the very first meeting that this woman had issues. Though I couldn't pinpoint it, it was quite obvious, yet the organization hired her "in the best interest of the child," jeopardizing a child's life by being in the care of an unstable caseworker.

I know people gossip, and a lot of gossip isn't necessarily the truth, but apparently there was some truth to the conversation, because all of a sudden it was as though the case worker disappeared. I never saw nor heard of her again, and, of course, no explanation was ever given about her whereabouts.

Neighbors

I USED TO read about deception, conspiracy involving others, and always had that ounce of doubt, the thought that perhaps the media exaggerated a bit. The thought never crossed my mind that such could happen to me. What I've learned is that we do live and learn, and we don't have the foggiest idea as to what the future holds.

It's amazing to what extreme people will go just to destroy another. It seemed impossible for my situation to get any worse, but to my surprise, it was continuous. Now it was grasping for straws, time to use any tactic necessary.

When the incident happened with my son, some of my neighbors whom we had been so kind to had become witnesses against us. The years I had lived in the neighborhood, I could count the people on one hand I knew personally. Others were acknowledged and greeted, but no socialization. Basically from the time I moved there, I was too involved with other obligations, responsibilities. I worked, I was in the military reserves, I was in college, and then later my son was born. I had little time to socialize with the majority of my neighbors, so they knew little to nothing about me. My son's father had only been a visitor prior to moving in after the birth of our son, so they knew even less about him.

I sat in court and later read how the HRS investigator had scouted the neighborhood not only trying to find negative information that could be used against us, but also was trying to recruit people to testify against us. I couldn't believe he had gone to such extremes to "build his case against us."

I'm not sure how many neighbors he tried to get involved to say negative things about us. Thank God there were some honest people who refused to lie. Unfortunately, there were some who decided to participate. It was puzzling; we had never had any problems with the neighbors. Many didn't even know our names. We were always polite; we would speak and basically tend to our business.

I did find out sometime later that the investigator was going around showing photos of a baby he claimed was mine. The information I received was the baby in the photo was shown without a face, only the badly bruised body, and also the baby was a dark skinned baby. Some who saw the photos knew it wasn't my fair, light-skinned baby. Others, after seeing such horrible photos and hearing the false accusations, perhaps felt as though they had an obligation to protect the child from the "child abusers" and perhaps feared for their own children as well.

I had befriended a couple of the neighbors, an older woman, and a woman around my age, the one I had the most contact with.

The older woman knew all the tenants and what went on in the neighborhood. She often met me as I exited the car to fill me in with the day's news, what some would call gossip. I didn't mind listening and talking with her. She was harmless, and I suppose somewhat lonely, though it did get somewhat difficult to continue this routine once I got pregnant.

I was attending college during the morning and working in the evening, leaving little time in between to get the much-needed rest my body demanded. I had to laugh at myself during the times I attempted to escape unsuccessfully. I would hurry from the car, make it to the door, and just as I would get the key in the lock, I'd hear that familiar voice. I knew from that moment I would get no rest that day.

I met the younger woman when I first moved into the neighborhood. She lived directly across the street from me. Before my life took a busy turn, we spend a great deal of time together. We often went out to dinner and social events. We did establish a friendship. It wasn't much that we didn't talk about. Eventually she met my son's father and had a good relationship with him. She was there all through my pregnancy; she would testify against me.

I was beyond surprised when HRS presented before the court information given to them by a couple of my neighbors, even statements given by the manager, stating my son's father was " intoxicated and belligerent" late one night.

In the years I had known him, I never witnessed such. He drank beer socially and not even in my presence. I never saw him drunk and definitely not belligerent. He seldom raised his voice. I thought this was unreal until I heard the next report from the investigator from another neighbor. He said the neighbor had complained to him about seeing my son's father kill a cat by smashing his head against the wall.

Although my attorney had addressed it briefly when she decided to represent only me, we didn't know the complete detail.

We looked at each other with the same shocking expression. He was almost speechless when he heard this. He could barely verbalize words to defend himself. He had so much compassion for animals and was especially fond of cats.

The lies were beginning to take an evil turn. This, of course, was to prove what a violent person he was. It has been documented that people who are cruel to animals are capable of doing the same to humans.

This so-called act of animal violence was just another block in our path used to continue to build a case. Although the accusation was applied toward him, it affected me indirectly. His actions were a reflection on me to indicate and justify my role in the abuse of our son.

This was the first time we had heard the full details of such accusations and wondered why the manager hadn't confronted us of such a hideous act before now.

We didn't have the slightest idea as to whom this woman was making such accusations. We were surprised to see a young woman called to the stand to testify. We soon recognized her as the young woman who lived to the far end of the complex, one that we always greeted in a friendly manner and never held any lengthy conversation with.

When the woman started to testify, she surprised us as well as the HRS lawyer and representatives by saying she never said such a thing about seeing my son's father killing a cat. Regardless of the lawyer's effort to get her to admit she had said so, she refused to do so. Before we could breathe a breath of relief, the HRS representative stated to the court the reason for the young woman's refusal to testify was that she was a single parent fearful of retaliation.

I must admit these people were quick in their thinking. They were determined to win, regardless of what extremes they had to go through. This woman was sworn under oath to tell the truth, and that's what she did .When I looked at her, I didn't see a woman engulfed with fear, but a woman trying to express herself, a woman baffled and surprised to hear of the accusation she was supposedly accusing us of; a woman who was simply trying to do the right thing by just telling the truth.

Betrayal of a Friend

WHEN I MOVED into the apartment complex, the woman who lived directly across the street from me came over to introduce herself. I was surprised when she told me she and my niece had worked together at one time.

She and I had something in common. We were both alone with no children, so that gave us the freedom to socialize without obligations, and I was able to do this before I started furthering my education.

We talked about many things, shared ideas, opinions, and met each other's family members, boyfriends. Before long, we had established a friendship. Eventually I went back to school and got pregnant. She was with me from the beginning to the end of my pregnancy and visited even more often after the birth of my son. When I went back to work earlier than planned, she was the one I trusted to babysit him for a day. After all, I had known her almost four years. She lived close by, and was with us enough to know how to take care of him.

I knew she wasn't a criminal; she was employed by the state, so she had a background check. Coincidently, she was an HRS employee, had been employed there for less than a year. She babysat my son on the day of the incident, so she knew in that eight-hour period, after holding him, changing him, that she observed no bruises on him.

So when we were accused of child abuse because of the "many bruises over my baby's body and some in various stages of healing;" according to the abuse report, which indicated there were prior bruises, there was a sense of relief knowing my friend and neighbor was a witness. She knew the truth. I thought this part of the investigation would be an open and shut case, but was I ever so wrong. Never in a hundred years would I have believed my friend would betray me.

When I realized that HRS was moving forward with accusations of abuse and was making a case out of it, I knew my friend would be caught in the middle of friendship and her job, so I never put her in that predicament. I didn't want to jeopardize her job, so, therefore, I had intentionally not mentioned anything about the case. I never tried to get her to take sides, to lie about anything. I didn't discuss anything with her concerning the case. I never thought to even worry about it; I just expected her to tell the truth. I knew by doing so everything would turn out fine.

The day of court, I was feeling nervous about everything else that was going on. I got consolation in knowing that at least one thing would be in our favor once my friend took the stand and let the truth be known.

When she was called to testify, she was nervous. I understood the feeling, but when she started to answer the HRS lawyer's questions, I was losing my understanding.

I couldn't believe what my ears were hearing. Of course, he made it known to the court that she was an HRS employee; perhaps this was also to remind her as well.

He proceeded to ask if we were friends. She answered,

"We're neighbors." When he asked if we socialized, "No, not lately." She answered as though we were complete strangers.

Over the years we had known each other, she visited me two to three times a week and sometimes even more. I thought perhaps she was trying to protect me in some way, but then as the questions and answers continued, I realized that wasn't it at all. She was trying to protect herself and her job. Every answer she gave was quite obvious answers to stay on the HRS' good side.

At one point, I almost felt pity for her, I think she realized what she was doing and felt badly, because she knew of the friendship we had, so she occasionally tried to tell the truth without elaborating as she did with most of her answers. "Did you ever see the baby's father with him?"

"Yes, twice." She paused. "He was in the room with him." She made it sound suspicious. When had it become a crime for a father to be in a room with his son?

She added, "When relatives were over, the father showed no affection toward the baby." I still couldn't figure this one out at the time, but later it would be used again in the building of the case.

Answers continued in this manner. She tried the same approach when questioned by my attorney. My attorney asked, "Did HRS ever contact you about the incident?"

"No, they didn't, but they may have, I don't have a telephone," yet she worked with them every day.

She was finally forced by the truth to answer directly, "Did you see any bruises on the baby the day you babysat him?" She nervously looked at the HRS lawyer, representatives. "No". After the questioning, she started to cry and ran out of the courtroom. She knew at that point she had destroyed our friendship.

I had mixed emotions; I was surprised at her actions, but

was hurt as well, that she would do something like this. I even tried to rationalize, tried to understand her fear of losing her job, but then I thought of myself, I never would have done such a thing. If the truth would have caused me my job, so be it, I am a believer that the truth prevails.

Needless to say, this indeed destroyed our friendship. I decided to move away, but before doing so, I wrote a letter to her telling her how I felt, how hurt I was that she would betray me that way, and made her aware of the things she said. I never gave her the letter, perhaps because of fear of it possibly being used against me in some way. I simply didn't trust her anymore. To be betrayed by a friend only added to my pain and suffering. I knew the friendship could never be rekindled.

The Doctor

IT WAS NOT only a transition for me, but for my baby as well. I had him established with his own pediatrician, but now that he was in the system, his doctors were appointed, people who knew nothing about him. What I found out was his doctor visits had nothing to do with him getting his check up or physicals, because even though they tried to exclude me from his life, I continued to keep track of his health, knowing when he needed his physicals and vaccines. I had to fight, had to involve my attorney for him to receive his vaccines. They weren't concerned about his well being; the visits to the doctors were strictly used for the building of the case.

After battling with the court, my sister finally had temporary custody of my son. During one of his doctor's appointments, I accompanied my sister to the doctor, he was unaware as to who I was. I sat, watched, and listened as he examined my baby, searching for evidence. He finally made a scandalous remark to my sister, a remark that took everything within me to keep quiet and not comment to try to defend myself to not make matters worse. He said, "This baby's mother used drugs."

My sister immediately responded to him and said, "This baby's mother is my sister, and she doesn't use drugs."

The doctor thought my sister was a foster mother under HRS, had no idea she was my baby's aunt. To my sister's and my surprise, the doctor then made the comment, "I'm just saying what I was told."

This was now becoming one big conspiracy; it was getting scary because I didn't know who or how many people were involved. Instead of this doctor doing an assessment and evaluation on his own, the outcome was predetermined.

After my sister confronted him about the situation, I noticed a slight change in his attitude, his behavior. I presented this to my attorney. I don't know what happened after this, but I don't remember him testifying in court. Perhaps from that day he chose not to be a part of it all, or perhaps he was overwhelmed with guilt or good old morals.

Strangers in the Night

THE DOCTOR WHO recommended my lawyer also suggested that I keep a journal of everything. I remembered him telling me that I would forget many things. He knew my emotional state. I took his advice. At the time, he had no idea just how helpful the journal would become.

I was desperate and seeking whatever help I could find. I wrote letters to the United States Senate, the Florida House of Representatives, and whomever else I could plead my case to. Needless to say, the health and rehabilitation service wasn't happy and was out to make my life even more miserable. However, I did receive responses from the letters I had written; the representative telling me he was forbidden to intervene in any case that goes before the courts and from the Senator a copy of the reply from the Department of Health and Rehabilitative Services. Their response was that the case was handled professionally in accordance with programmatic rules and regulations and basically we were child abusers.

I did appreciate that the matter was looked into. Time passed. I had no sense of time anymore. It was difficult to remember one day to the next, and I did, however, continue to write in my journal. I was in and out of court with more negative results than positive.

My son's father and I received a call one day telling us to meet in my attorney's office. The meeting was at night. I took my journal along with me. When we got there, three men, all dressed in suits, introduced themselves.

I have no remembrance of who they were. I think one introduced himself as someone dealing with civil rights. No one knew at the time who had sent the men nor their purpose for being there, the health and rehabilitative service staff or my attorney.

I found out the men had been investigating and interviewing different people throughout that day. The men were pleasant, with a different personality from what we had experienced.

For the first time through this whole ordeal, it seemed as though someone cared and would finally listen. They talked with us, asked questions. I told them I kept a journal; they asked if they could take it. The men finished their interview and, as quickly as they arrived, they were gone.

Somehow, after talking with these men, I had a feeling of hope. I felt as though they were honestly trying to find the truth, and in doing so would realize that something unlawful and unethical was involved in my case.

From the night the strangers disappeared, I never heard from them again, but felt they had some bearing on the outcome of my case. I don't know what transpired or what influence they had in getting my son back, but I do know some time later things begin to change. Eventually, I was even appointed a new Judge.

The Exchange

WHEN ALL EVIDENCE confirmed that my case was indeed racially based, my attorney decided to file a lawsuit, not only due to racism, but also for procedures not being followed nor standard rules for investigating child abuse. The suit not only asked for monetary damages, but also to get my son back and to stop the harassment.

When the media made this known to the public, different lawyers then wanted to take the case to file for a larger amount than my attorney sued for. I had no interest whatsoever. What good is money without happiness, and I had no happiness without my son. I wanted my son to come home. No amount of money could fulfill that void.

One day I received a call from my attorney's office to meet her to discuss the lawsuit. Under my attorney's advice, I signed papers to drop the lawsuit. It was like an exchange; if I drop the lawsuit, I would get my son back, so this was what I did with no questions asked, even to this day.

Psychologist II

ALMOST A YEAR had passed. Although I had my son back, I was still battling with the court for closure of the case and needed some closure in my life.

I was so "normal" before this nightmare began, contrary to the belief of those who tried to destroy my life by labeling me with mental disorders.

I suppose it was somewhat ironic, because now I actually suffered from adjustment disorder with mixed emotions. It was as though the emotions that had been stored away inside me, which were forbidden to surface because of fear, control, powerlessness, finally crossed those barriers and presented themselves in a manner even frightening to me.

When I was in nursing school, we discussed Dr. Kubler Ross' five stages of grief model. She wrote a book titled *On Death and Dying*. She discussed emotional states referred to as the grief cycle. The stages were denial, anger, bargaining, depression, and acceptance.

These were the process she spoke of that people go through when dealing with death, but later realized her theory didn't only apply to the dying process, but with any type of grief and tragedy.

She stated they don't necessarily come in order, and one

may not experience them all, but will experience at least two, even switching between stages.

I was now going through the stages of my loss. One day while I was unaware of my transition into another stage, I found myself angry, something I had not allowed myself to experience. Each time before, when the anger tried to break through, depression, sadness, fear would immediately dominate, and anger submissively subsided. Anger started to mingle with fear. My mind started to race. I started reliving the nightmare, and then started to think of the possibility of it happening again. I visualized going through the pain of losing my son again, and scary thoughts entered my mind. I knew I couldn't let them take him again. I knew I wouldn't live through it again.

I immediately sought help, searching for a Psychologist, anyone qualified to help me at this point. I had no idea who to call, so I searched the pages of the telephone book and chose a woman Psychologist who counseled individuals as well as family.

I had no idea what the woman would be like or if she would be just as prejudiced and biased as the previous Psychologist. My trust level was down to zero. I wasn't sure whom I could trust anymore, and, after all, a friend had even betrayed me.

When I finally met with the counselor, I experienced good vibes. This special gift of mine seldom steered me wrong. She was a pleasant woman and had already heard about my case, which was no surprise since it had been front-page news, broadcast and televised. It didn't take her long to realize that the case indeed was racially based. In one of our sessions, it was difficult for her to maintain her professionalism by not shedding tears. I watched as she fought back the tears. She asked me with such empathy in her voice, "Why don't you just move away?"

I suppose as fearful as I was, knowing these people basically had control of my life, I was not going to run away. I was going to somehow gain control of my life again and was going to do it here in this town, in this county where I grew up. This was my home; I was not going to let hate and prejudice run me out of town.

After three sessions, the Psychologist agreed that rapport was easily established. The therapy sessions were going well, then one day, as the Psychologist wrote in her report, she received a call from an HRS worker who insisted on coming to her office to discuss my case. The Psychologist told the worker she had no release signed to talk to her. The worker told her that there was a court order that stated that there was no confidentiality in respect to my case. I couldn't begin to describe my feelings. I wondered when the nightmare was going to end, if ever.

There were true cases of child abuse happening all around, yet so much money and time were spent on my case, even after the investigation proved there was no proof of child abuse and all attempts failed in building a case. Since they weren't able to achieve their goal in destroying me in one way, they were trying another approach.

I was surprised to read in the Psychology report that there was a recognition that I couldn't get on with my life until this nightmare was over. She, too, described this as a nightmare.

Things started getting out of control. She started getting calls, visits from the HRS workers, Guardian ad litem- an advocate for a child whose welfare is a matter of concern for the court. She specifically encouraged me to discontinue counseling with her while my case was still open to HRS supervision.

She wrote in her assessment that I had adjustment reactions to the circumstances at hand. She assessed me to be a fully responsible and loving parent who needed support and the ability to express my anger and frustrations.

She also stated that she did not believe it was fair to encourage me to do so with her, in that our therapeutic relationship has already been contaminated by the HRS insistence in talking to her, as well as the Guardian ad litem, reiterating that there was a court order which stated that there was no confidentially with respect to my case. Therefore, any communication we had in our therapy together was subject to review from the courts.

She stated she would not, based on the situation, want to be involved in a professional therapeutic relationship based on these circumstances either. I did cease all sessions with her, as suggested.

I received a copy of the report and progress notes sent. In it, the Psychologist wrote how the HRS worker came to her office with no documentation to present to her and how her overall attitude and statements suggested that there was grave concern about my son being physically abused. She also wrote how she met with the Guardian ad item, which had a completely different attitude toward my situation. She didn't believe that my baby was in any danger and asked her to submit a report on my behalf. She also at that time showed her the court order at which there was no indication that counseling was ordered.

She had done her best to assure me that she was my advocate and was willing to help in any way that she possibly could and wanted to discontinue our therapy until such time as I would feel more comfortable with the more "customary confidentially standards of private therapy."

It was as though everyone who tried to help me soon themselves became targets. I decided to end counseling completely, even after my case was officially closed. I told the Psychologist the only way I would find closure was to write about my nightmare. Writing had always been therapeutic for me since childhood. I've always found that expressing myself on paper, what I call transfer therapy, allows me to transfer my feelings and thoughts elsewhere,

therefore leaving me with a peace of mind. Also, this was a place where my privacy couldn't be invaded.

Breaking of the Bond

NO ONE WOULD ever know the pain of having the bond broken between a mother and a child unless one has experienced it. It is similar to the gripping pain a woman experiences in childbirth, just involves a different part of the body, the heart. I'm sure many women will agree when I say that the bond is formed long before birth.

During my pregnancy, I would visualize and daydream about my baby. I would imagine him in the car seat while I was driving, just involving him in my everyday life. I would even read to him, play music for him, so needless to say, when he was born, the bond was strong, perhaps more so than most. No doubt, this was why I felt that something was wrong with him on the night he had fallen from the bed.

I don't know if I would ever be able to find a word in the dictionary to define the way I felt when my baby was taken from me. I wanted to die because I felt that it was impossible to live without him and to live with so much grief, but a part of me knew I had to live for my baby. My twin had lost a child. I remembered her saying to me, "At least you will get your child back." I was experiencing so much grief that I lost my ability to think rationally. Only for a brief moment after hearing those words from my sister was I able to shift my grief on to her, realizing the loss she had was permanent, and the pain she must have endured was beyond unbearable.

Unfortunately, I wasn't able to stay in the shifted state for too long. My mind drifted back, and my heart again was engulfed with fear of the unknown, thoughts of the possibility of losing my son forever.

Although this ordeal had several painful moments, I think the most painful of all was losing control over my child's life. At one moment, I had full control. I decided when I wanted to feed him, bathe him, take him for a stroll, play with him, or whatever it was I needed to do with him, to losing complete control.

I will never forget how I was treated, disrespected. It's strange how people judge someone from other people's perception of a person without really knowing that person.

It's so easy for people to believe something negative about someone. I feel that when people focus on that negative, they don't allow themselves to see the good in that person, so therefore a negative attitude is projected toward that person.

I experienced such an attitude first-hand. It was bad enough having to deal with my son's medical care being switched from his private pediatrician, which I had provided for him, to him going to a public clinic where no one knew anything about him nor his history, but what was worse was the day I accompanied my sister to the clinic.

I was overlooked and ignored by the person examining him as though I didn't exist. The person had no interest whatsoever in what I had to say. All I wanted was to make sure my baby was getting the proper care, but the attitude projected toward me was, if I had to put it in words, "You are a criminal, a child abuser, you don't have a say or any rights."

She looked through me as though I was transparent. She

would direct her questions to my sister without making eye contact with me, making it quite obvious that she was ignoring me. I knew everything there was to know about my baby, but even my rights to share that information were taken away, and these people were supposed to be doing what was in the "best interest of the child."

After the Fact

I WAS SO focused on reuniting with my son until it never occurred to me that I was also facing other serious issues. One day it was brought to my attention by the organization and my attorney that there was the possibility of going to jail, criminal charges being filed. Fortunately, because of lack of evidence of child abuse, the investigator and the organization were unable to pursue the charges. Even through all the effort of trying to build a case and false accusations, no signs of child abuse could be found.

I actually never allowed myself to stress over this matter, perhaps because I was so mentally and physically drained, and I had no more energy to spare, or perhaps my faith assured me that the good Lord would intervene before such drastic measures would take place.

Another issue was the possibility of the suspension of my nursing license. This was, indeed, a major issue. This was my livelihood, my means of providing for my son, something I had made sacrifices for and worked so hard to obtain.

My job was working with elderly patients, something I enjoyed, going to work each day with hope that I had made a difference in their lives. If my license were taken away, not only would I not be allowed to work with these elderly patients anymore, but no patients of any age, especially children.

It is truly a black mark to be presented before the board of nursing as an abuser. Not only is it a crime, but as nurses, we have a code of conduct we as professionals are expected to abide by, and we are expected to conduct ourselves in a professional manner. Thank God, I had great support from my employer, co-workers, doctors, family, and friends who wrote letters and spoke on my behalf. I didn't have to appear before the board and was able to maintain my license.

It just amazes me how a mind could be so emotionally traumatized that a person seems to go into a state of amnesia. I never thought of this type of reaction as being real, a recognizable disorder; I just knew it happened to me. Then, years later, I was watching television and, to my surprise, a medical professional educated in this area addressed this condition. There was a young man being discussed with this condition. Unfortunately, the young man's condition was severe. He had lost his memory completely. Something so traumatic had happened to him that it totally erased his memory.

As time passed, it seemed as though I remembered less and less. I'm not sure if I intentionally stored the painful memories in my subconscious mind and just not allowed them to surface, or if this was some type of defense mechanism, something inborn to protect my sanity. Perhaps I was in a state of denial or just overwhelmed from all the stress so much that it had just taken its toll.

What did remain in my memory was the day and the only day my mother waited for me in the court lobby. I've often heard that history repeats itself. I'm not sure specifically what type of history, but again I watched as my mother sat haplessly once more by my side with sadness in her eyes as I was being falsely accused, just as I had been some twenty or so years previously.

She had always been our protector. Now her eyes, her body position, let me know that she was now facing another situation where she was powerless. Although this was a difficult time for me, I felt sadness as I watched her. She had no power or control over the situation just as it was years ago. The only thing she was able to offer then and now was love and support.

I knew only too well the pain a mother suffers for the sake of her child. Perhaps my tears were not only for myself but for her as well. It saddened me to see her much older now with her lack of control of the situation. Although she was living in another era with hopes of changing times, I knew the memories of racism continued to haunt her.

After that day, she never walked into the courtroom again. I knew the only room she felt she could go to was the room we were familiar with, her room, to pray.

It's sad and scary to know that there are people who hold high positions and possess great power who are aware of the many issues and wrong doing that goes on in this country, yet make little to no effort to correct it. I'm a firm believer that one day we will all reap what we sow.

My mother reminded us throughout our childhood into adulthood that what happens in the dark would one day come to the light.

I was so mentally drained and physically exhausted after going through my nightmare that it never occurred to me as to what really happened with the investigation from the unknown men from the state capitol or what was happening period. I suppose by trying to store away so many of the unpleasant memories, my mind would only let me focus on one thing, being with my son.

It wasn't until months later that I heard from a state work-er, of course, something I wasn't to be aware of, about the publicity and the secret changes my case brought about.

Throughout my case, my lawyer brought forth evidence that pointed toward racism, but the state lawyer and workers would never admit such and managed to focus on issues to steer away from the topic. Now I heard from this worker, who finally admitted to me that she knew my son had not been abused, but she didn't have the courage to speak up, that it became mandatory that state workers attended a class on racism, and she told me my case was the topic, the example used.

I suppose my emotions were mixed; I was angry- angry because they made us suffer needlessly, especially my son, angry because they labeled us with psychological disorders to justify the abuse that never happened, angry because I was falsely accused. I was sad because of what my son went through, the broken bond, the things and time we can't re-kindle. Sad because issues could have been resolved quickly, when the truth was there from the very beginning, preventing the nightmare from happening, and then happy because the darkness came to light, because maybe someone would listen and learn and take action to prevent the same thing from hap-pening again to someone else.

I also found out the man responsible for the nightmare was secretly transferred. Then I started to exhibit the same mixed emotions, except a new one entered the picture, fear-fear because I know a tiger doesn't change his stripes. Evil was ingrained in this man. I was not the first victim and doubt if I would be the last. I feared wherever he went, his evil and prejudice would surface again.

Fear

EVEN TODAY AS I look back, I ask myself, would I have raised my son differently had I not gone through this nightmare? Would I be a different mother than the one I am today? Over protective would be the term to describe my behavior.

I remember when my son was perhaps around two years old he was spinning around in the living room and no doubt had gotten dizzy from doing so. He fell into the glass table I had centered in the middle of the floor, hitting his nose on the corner of the table. I experienced immediate fear. Although it was just a little bleeding from his nose, the fear was overwhelming. From that time on my son was shielded, protected from falls, any scraps, or cuts. I didn't allow him to play in the sand; I was like a bodyguard when he was at play. When he finally started riding his bicycle, kneepads, elbow pads covered his skin and, of course, a helmet covered his head.

I feel at times that I deprived him of a normal childhood. It dawned on me one day that my son didn't have the childhood scars that children usually sustain from falling, whether from riding their bicycles or from just simply running around playing. I never allowed him to fall, was always there watching, protecting him, I was so afraid to let him play, as other children did, fear of him falling and hurting himself.

I never even allowed him to sleep alone for many years. Even with him sleeping with me, I would wake several times throughout the night to check him. Though I've come a long way, I don't think I or others who have experienced what I have will ever heal completely and, if so, it will take a long time.

At first I consciously lived in fear of him being taken again, fear of something happening to him. As the years passed, I thought I had conquered my fear, only to realize that it had become an unconscious fear to the point where I wasn't certain anymore of what my fear entailed. I suppose it was an embedded fear of losing him. I think perhaps I just gained more control of the fear.

When my son was around the age of eleven, he ran into the house with a scraped knee, telling me he had fallen off his bicycle. What I noticed was he wasn't crying. It was almost excitement. For the first time I nursed his wound without fear. Deep inside I believe I rejoiced somewhat, knowing that he finally had the opportunity to fall off his bicycle, and I was able to respond to his needs without having a panic attack. I believe he, too, felt that freedom. There was now hope and the possibility of him being free to start living a normal life.

I just hoped and prayed that it hadn't affected my son in any way as he got older. He did tell me some years later how he felt being the only child not being able to participate in activities during certain field trips when he was in elementary and even in middle school. I feared every time he went on a field trip that something would happen to him. I went on the field trips I was able to go on; the others I hoped and prayed each time and got no peace of mind until he returned. The one field trip he spoke of and remembered so vividly was the rock climbing. Fear definitely got the best of me.

I was so afraid that he would fall and hurt himself that I refused to sign a consent form for him to participate. I even contacted a lawyer concerning the consent and terms of the agreement of the consent. I wasn't comfortable with what the consent entailed. Therefore, I made the decision not to let him go. His teacher told me that he would be the only one left in the classroom. I agreed for him to go, but not participate in the activity. I knew it was unfair to him. He told me how he had to sit and watch the other children as they participated.

I knew I had to make some changes and learn to conquer my fear. Through the years it has gotten better. I would like to think now the fear, or perhaps worry will be a better word, that I have is just normal, something that is a natural part of being a mother.

Effect

ALTHOUGH THE YEARS have passed, unfortunately the dreadful memories linger. I still find myself crying at times when I talk and think about the nightmare, especially when I think of the things and time I can never rekindle.

My son was four months old when I was finally reunited with him. I think back on the things that I missed that some people take for granted, such as not being able to take my son to get his first shots. In my life plan, I had looked forward to the day of taking him to get his first shot. I haven't the slightest idea who took him, nor his reaction, only that I know I had to fight to get it done. This was my only opportunity; there will never be another first. Something that seems so insignificant to someone else was so important to me.

However, the hurt that will remain with me is not knowing about the care he received and what really happened to him while he was out of my care. I think how meticulous I was with his overall care, which explains why I was beyond upset one day while we were at visitation.

During this time my son was in foster care, as I awaited for his arrival, the foster woman entered the room without him, instead, a child under the age of twelve, which I gathered to be another foster child, walked in carrying him. Never would I have allowed a child to hold my baby. In addition, to make matters worse, he was filthy; vomitus was all over his clothes.

At that moment, I knew my son was not being taken care of properly. If they presented him in public and at the health and rehabilitation building this way, how were they treating him at foster care? I will never forget the helpless feeling. I had absolutely no control nor say so. All I could do was cry. I knew at that moment I had to work harder to get my baby out of foster care.

The effect of this nightmare is never ending. I find myself constantly living it in some form. I can compare it when people are diagnosed with certain diseases or have dealt with other crises and how it changes their lives.

Many become supporters, either forming or become part of support groups or organizations, and then all of a sudden it becomes a part of their lives. They are much aware of any issues that pertain to their circumstances.

I find myself in a similar situation, though I'm not sure if it's positive or negative. To this day, my heart still goes out to the people accused of child abuse. While many people immediately, after hearing the news from the media, pass judgment on these people, the first question that appears in my mind is, have these people been falsely accused?

A part of me battles with this, and I feel somewhat guilty by not allowing myself to immediately focus on the child. At one point, I feared my judgment had been morally jeopardized from the nightmare I have experienced, but after analyzing, I realized it is nothing morally wrong in waiting and searching for the truth before basing my opinion and making a judgment.

Being a victim will not allow me to jump to conclusions. I

simply must know the truth. I know what it's like to be falsely accused. The accuser not only suffers, but the child/children as well. It is not until the truth unfolds that I base my opinion. It is only at this point where my heart shifts and goes out to the children, knowing the suffering they will endure emotionally from their loss as well. Many people don't take the time to realize that many children are affected.

This had an effect on the relationship between my son and his father. He grew up without his father being a part of his life. The investigator and other members of the organization were successful in part of what they set out to do- separate us.

I remember being called to the school one day when my son was in elementary. He was crying and upset because another student asked about his father. Throughout his childhood, he would cry on occasion, asking for his father.

At one point, his father and I were forced to separate and basically have no contact with each other after my son was reunited with me. We were still being watched, especially me. We were not going to jeopardize losing our son again by having any contact as part of the agreement.

His father moved to another county and understood to some degree about the risk of my losing him again. It was difficult for him to understand why, since there was neither evidence nor charges of child abuse against either of us. However, we had fought a long losing battle with racism. No reason was needed, and this was the way it was for now.

There was no energy or will left in me, especially to fight anymore. I had won the biggest fight of getting my son back.

We were being watched as though we were criminals. They were just waiting for the opportunity for us to make a mistake, but it was not going to happen.

I never knew when they finally stopped watching, perhaps a year or longer, but during that time my son's father didn't see him, and he would only have contact via phone. When the case was finally closed, unfortunately, we weren't able to rekindle the relationship; therefore, they never had the opportunity to establish that father and son relationship.

I was waiting for the right time to explain to my son why his father was not a part of his life, waiting for the right age for him to understand the society we were living in. I wanted him to be old enough to talk to him about racism in a way that he wouldn't be bitter or angry. I wanted him to be able to understand that people are not bad by race, that there are people in every race who make bad choices, not to stereotype as we had been, to be proud of who he is and accept people for who they are. I hid newspaper articles, journals, any information that pertain to him being taken away.

During his teenage years, the gap widened between him and his father. Though his father started to make more contact via phones and visits, my son distanced himself. I knew he had mixed emotions, one being anger at his father for not being a part of his life.

I finally sat down with him and told him when he was sixteen. I think perhaps I kept avoiding the issue because I didn't know the approach to take or how he would react. What really triggered my telling him one day was when he made me aware of my strictness, my over- protectiveness. I felt at that moment it was time to explain my behavior and why his father had been an absent parent. I also knew he had matured and had enough diversity in his life. He had attended a private school for ten years, then a public school for the remainder of high school. I wanted him to be able to socialize with people of all different races, cultures, and economical backgrounds.

I had taught him that people are individuals and cannot be stereotyped nor classed by race as good or bad, therefore to restrain from thinking all white people are prejudiced, racist, and evil because of what happened in our lives. Accept the fact that, though we were all created equal in God's sight, there are still those and perhaps always will be those who don't believe in equality, who have the superiority complex, believing that others are inferior. I knew he was ready for the truth.

I had always been able to give him a rational answer to his questions, but this time when he asked about racism and why this happened, there was no rational answer to give. Racism cannot be justified.

Through my imperfection, just part of being human, I was not completely capable of refraining from judging others, jumping to conclusions. I believed everything I read or heard prior to my nightmare. Now I know what it is like to be misrepresented, to be falsely accused, to be criticized, so therefore I've gained something positive from a bad or negative situation and have learned a valuable lesson as well, and that is to not believe everything that I read nor hear until there is some verification.

I continue to read, to watch documentaries, and some movies that are not too emotional, many times with tears streaming down my cheeks about families being torn apart. I watch children yelling and screaming for their parents as they are being taken away.

This horrible act has been going on for years. I watched sadly while some children were taken away from their parents because the parents were poor, food was scarce. Some had no jobs, no decent place to live, and many other reasons that had nothing to do with child abuse in the sense.

Society has taken the same approach for years- take the children. How can a country be so civilized, so"free," with so many educated leaders, psychological experts, not realized the devastated effect? There is often a short and long-term effect on both parent and child when a child is uprooted from his parents, environment, and family.

Such traumatic experiences follow many children throughout their childhood, their lives. When the children are young, the system claim they are doing what is in the best interest of the children, passing them from foster home to foster home, many without the love and nurturing that only parents can give.

Once the child is an older teenager or young adult, they no longer qualify for foster care. The system does not support them anymore; they are basically on their own. Many end up on the street and become part of the system in a different way, behind prison walls. Many in prison have a story behind their lives. There is a correlation between foster home and prison.

I know there are some extreme cases of child abuse where it is necessary to remove children from the home, but for the cases where there is still hope; there are other alternatives simple enough that it doesn't take a rocket scientist to figure. Why not provide food, shelter, education? Not only is it a wise ethical decision, but a wise economical one as well. So much money is spent putting a child through the system when it could be used for measures to keep the family together and to prevent another mother's nightmare.

Racism

I REALIZED AS my case went on it wasn't so much about my son's alleged abuse, because it was quite obvious he was not. No test or physical evidence confirmed it. He was a happy, healthy baby. It was because of racism. I was being punished because I crossed the color barrier. Not only did the lead player, the racist investigator, play a major part, he had other participants. It was as though he was the scout. Once he found one who broke the rule, dating interracially, that unfortunate person became the prey. He had the followers to back him up, even the judge who made it known that he did not approve of interracial relationships. Many people played a role in this unethical scheme.

From the moment I walked into the emergency room with my son, I was not given a ghost of a chance. I was a single black woman with a child. From there the assumption began. It was assumed that I was uneducated and ignorant. When the emergency room doctor decided to admit my baby more so for suspicion of child abuse, I was appointed a pediatrician. It was assumed right away that I had no insurance, that I was another welfare case, another topic often related to the black race.

in fact, while we were at a deposition hearing my lawyer

asked an HRS worker, "Why didn't you all talk to her pediatrician and gynecologist?"

The worker stated, "She told us she was going to the health department."

Statistics are one thing, but stereotyping is another. I know statistics, profiling, all of these things have their place and can be a reliable resource at certain times and for certain situations, but not always a hundred percent accurate. There are times when one just does not fit the profile. I was just another statistic; these so-called experts looked into my eyes, listened to my voice, interpreted my words, then concluded that I fit the profile as a child abuser.

Although I have suffered in the worst way, something I wish no mother would ever have to go through, I cannot let bitterness control my life. I found, through suffering I have gained strength.

I am a strong believer in the famous phrases *What goes around comes around, Unjust does not prosper, We will reap what we sow.*

I continue to see people as individuals and refuse to stereotype; after all, I have been a victim and know first-hand what it's like to be judged because of race, skin color, and economic background.

I would like to think that when people are racist, there is a stopping point he or she reaches that allows him/her to search for some possible embedded morals.

I will forever wonder if the racist HRS worker who took my son that night actually abused him in any way. After all, he was trying to build a case, and he did take some extreme measures in trying to do so. I just don't know to what extreme.

Unlike many fads, designs that have come and gone, technologies that have brought about changes, racism has lingered on throughout the years. It has been around for hundreds, perhaps thousands, of years and has always brought along with it hate and destruction. Racism is like a horrible disease. It possesses the same characteristics. It attacks every aspect of the body and mind and is capable of destroying. If we as a nation, a world, don't find a way to control it, it will become like an infectious disease, pandemic-an epidemic that is widespread, and eventually destroy us all in one way or another. Unlike many diseases, no research is needed to find the cause of racism, because the cause is insignificant. We just need to find the cure.

The Lake Sentinel

An Edition of The Orlando Sentinel

Suit: HRS unfair to biracial couple

A Leesburg woman says racism on the part of a child-abuse investigator has cost her the custody of her child.

By ....
OF THE SENTINEL STAFF

TAVARES — A Leesburg woman charges in a suit that she was unfairly targeted for a child abuse investigation by a racist investigator who was angry because the father of her child is white.

Brenda Avant, a black registered nurse says in the suit that she wants her 4-month-old baby boy back, she wants the state Department of Health and Rehabilitative Services to stop harassing her, and she wants more than $..... in damages.

The suit, filed late Monday afternoon in state Circuit Court in Lake County, also names HRS child abuse investigator ....

The lawsuit claims that at one point during the abuse investigation, ... told a social worker to back off the case and not do anything to help the couple because it involved "a white man living

off a black woman."

The suit, filed for Avant by attorney .... also charges that HRS and......

• Didn't follow standard rules for investigating child abuse.

• Didn't follow procedures to place the child with relatives instead of foster parent, although other workers later arranged for the child to live with relatives.

• Took no action when Avant's live-in boyfriend volunteered to leave the home until the abuse investigation was finished.

Here is how the case developed, according to the suit and those who filed it:

Avant and her boyfriend, became parents of a baby boy on June 5.

On July 24, Avant left the baby in the care of the father while she ran down the street to pick up a car from one of her nieces.

While she was gone, the baby fell from the bed and hit his face on the floor.

"He was scooting a lot," Avant said in an interview Tuesday. "Every once in a while, he would flip over, but he was mostly scooting around."

Avant took the baby to the hospital.

Please see HRS, 5

HRS questioned investigator, suit says

HRS'from 1

where doctors called in abuse investigators, as they routinely do when children are injured and emergency room personnel aren't satisfied with the caretaker's explanation.

.... was the investigator on call.

..............wouldn't respond to a telephone call Tuesday. A woman identifying herself as his secretary referred all questions to a district HRS office in Gainesville.

.........has worked for HRS since Sept. 5,' 1989, and moved to. Lake County from ......after asking for a transfer. He has received excellent work reviews, HRS officials said.

After the baby was admitted to the hospital he was treated by his pediatrician, who said he did not believe any abuse occurred and would not have called HRS, the suit alleges. But...... had the infant transferred to Shands Hospital in Gainesville. ...... said Tuesday the baby wasn't taken to Shands for treatment from the fall, but because........ wanted the child examined by a specialist to see if the baby had been abused." They found nothing, not the slightest indication." The baby was then transferred to a shelter home. When questioned, ... told colleagues that

he kept the child in shelter care to "build his case" against Avant, the suit alleges.

The suit further contends that Avant and her boyfriend were called into HRS headquarters in Tavares and interviewed by a foster care worker.

The worker, who is not identified by name, later asked.......... why he had not followed proper rules and checked "into placing the child with relatives, the suit says.-

Again, ... said he wanted time to gather more evidence against the mother, the suit states.

"............ further told her that she should not be supportive of this couple because it was 'a white man living off of a black woman,'" the suit alleges.'

.... spokeswoman, for HRS, said she is uncertain if such a remark was ever made, but said if it was it was improper.

"That is a totally inappropriate remark,"..... said. "There can be no justification for such a statement

.............decided on his own that the relationship between Avant and her boyfriend was "unstable and was subject to additional and extreme stress because of the fact that there was an interracial relationship and a biracial child," the suit stated.

........listed the biracial couple as a "stressor" for the child, and an HRS term for a stress-causing situation that could lead to child abuse, the suit alleges.

SUIT

Continued from A1

In fact, the suit says, the agency is harassing B.A. by claiming she used drugs during her pregnancy. She didn't, the suit says.

"Either............ is acting out-side of the guidelines, or HRS has developed a totally racist policy." ....said Monday. "This kind of ' attitude, to me, is a problem."

........is asking a judge to order HRS to return the child to B.A. She is also asking for an unspecified amount of damages.

Couple sue HRS in Lake

Suit says racism present in child-custody case

Daily Commercial Staff Writer

A Lake County couple is suing the state Department of Health and Rehabilitative Services, claiming that a caseworker took 'their 3-month-old baby into custody and won't return the infant because the mother is black and the father is white.

The suit was filed in Lake County, circuit court late Monday by Tavares attorney........, who used only initials to identify the' parents. HRS officials could not be reached for comment Monday.

According to the suit, the baby was injured July 21 when the baby fell off a bed. At the time of the fall, the .child's father — identified; in the suit as B.J.W. — was alone in the house with the child

The suit does not say how extensive the injuries were, but does say the child was taken to Shands Hospital in Gainesville, where he remained for several days.

During the hospital stay, HRS caseworker........ decided the case qualified as child abuse and began proceedings to take the, baby away from B.J.W. and B.A. the child's mother. When the child left Shands, the baby was placed in foster care.

But HRS was ignoring its own policies,"-........said in the suit. Several relatives of the ' mother contacted HRS and asked that the baby be placed with them while the abuse case was pending, but those requests were at first denied by........, the suit say.

When another caseworker tried to investigate the possibility of placing the child with relatives. .... told the caseworker to cease, saying he needed to "build his case" against the child's natural parents, the suit, says.

Later, ...told the same caseworker — identified only as "caseworker one" — that she should not be supportive of this couple because it was a "white man living off a black woman," the suit says. ', - - -

The suit also alleges that the natural father offered to move out of the couple's home if the child could be returned to his mother. HRS didn't even investigate the possibility of re turning the' child to the mother, the suit claims, despite the lack of abuse allegations against her.

Please see SUIT, A3

Woman may get child back

Leesburg couple's suit claims HRS prejudiced

By ....
Daily Commercial Staff Writer

TAVARES

A Leesburg woman who has charged state health officials with taking her baby because she's black and the father is white hopes to be reunited with her 4-month-old son this weekend her attorney said Wednesday.

Brenda Avant, claims in her suit that state Department of Health and Rehabilitative Services officials are keeping her away from her child because the couple is biracial.

> *"We're hoping we can resolve this matter quickly.'*
>
> **Tavares attorney**

Tavares attorney,...... who represents Avant, said she expects to meet with an HRS official this weekend "We're hoping we can resolve this matter quickly,..... said.

The child was taken into HRS custody nearly two months ago when he fell off a bed and bruised his head, the suit says. At the time of the child's injury, the father — who is named only as B.J.W. in the suit — was in sole charge of the child.

The child was taken to Shands Hospital in Gainesville, where he remained for several days, the suit said. During that time, caseworker.....
.... determined the child might have been a victim of abuse and took the baby into protective custody.

But..... .... violated HRS policies by putting the child into a foster home instead of checking out the possibility of placing the child with one of the woman's relatives,.......said. According to the suit, she commented to another caseworker — identified only as "Caseworker 1" in the suit — that he wanted to "build his case" against the baby's parents.

..... is withholding the caseworker's identity because the worker is afraid of retaliation by HRS hierarchy. However, ... lauded the wom-

an Wednesday for coming forward and saying she thought...... . handled the case inappropriately........ also told Caseworker 1 that she should not be supportive of the couple because it was a "white man living off a black woman," the suit says.

Avant said Wednesday that she thinks ..., ...'s handling of her case was heavily colored by racial prejudice.

"I sort of knew from the beginning," said the soft-spoken nurse. "But it took awhile for it to dawn on me."

In an attempt to get her baby back, Avant made .... an offer: The father of the child — the only person suspected of abuse — would move out if the child could be returned to Avant.

.......refused. Instead, the suit contends, he launched allegations against Avant, claiming she had used drugs during her pregnancy.

It was only through the intervention of the unidentified Caseworker 1 that the child was placed with one of Avant's relatives. But soon after the child was placed, HRS officials started to investigate the relative, claiming the child wasn't receiving proper medical care.

"Brenda is a model mother,". ..... said. "That's what makes this so outrageous."

Caseworker 1 told .... that the case was given much more attention than such cases usually receive, the suit says.

Tuesday, HRS officials said they hadn't seen the lawsuit. But HRS policies don't discriminate against interracial couples — unless something about the relationship acts as a "stressor," said ...., Please see SUIT, A7

SUIT

Continued from A1

spokeswoman for HRS.

"Clearly, race is not an issue," ...... said.

But in any case of suspected child abuse, the first priority is protecting the child,..... said.

In the suit, Avant asks that her child be returned immediately and that the court order HRS to stop its investigation and "harassment." The suit also asks for more than $..... in damages.

Her first priority is getting her baby back, Avant said. But she'd also like to see some evaluation of ......'s status.

"I don't think people should be in a position to work with children if they can't control their prejudices," Avant said. "They need to work a machine if they can't deal with people.

"I know child abuse has to be investigated, but there has to be another way. I don't think innocent parents should be allowed to suffer like I did."

A7